C000257679

THE LOUVRE

Objets d'Art

THE LOUVRE

Objets d'Art

Jannic Durand
Curator, Department of Objets d'Art

Introduction by Daniel Alcouffe
General Curator
Department of Objets d'Art

ZWEMMER
in association with RMN

Jacket illustration:
Pierre Delabarre, *Ewer*, c. 1630 (detail)
Endpapers:
Galerie d'Apollon

Designed by Jérôme Faucheux
Translated from the French by Judith Hayward
Printed in Italy by Graphicom

© 1995 Éditions Scala

First published in 1995 by Zwemmer, an imprint of Philip Wilson Publishers Ltd
28 Litchfield Street London WC2H 9NJ

Distributed in the USA and Canada by Antique Collectors' Club Ltd
Market Street Industrial Park, Wappingers Falls
NY 12500 USA

All rights Reserved

ISBN: 0 302 00675 3

CONTENTS

Introduction:
The Department of Objets d'Art

The Department of Objets d'Art looks very different from any other museum devoted to *objets d'art*. Rather than setting out to mirror the development of the disciplines associated with what are commonly known as the decorative or applied arts in an encyclopaedic manner, it illustrates some of these disciplines by means of works that have special significance, because they are early, or because of their exceptional quality or historical importance. Most come from the periods and countries that exemplify the art in question best: ivory and enamel from the Middle Ages, bronze and majolica from the Italian Renaissance, porcelain and French furniture from the eighteenth century. This may result from the way the Department's collections were formed, empirically rather than systematically.

The decree issued by the Convention on 27 July 1793 creating the Louvre museum anticipated that not only pictures and statues but "vases" and "precious furniture" too would be brought there, from the former royal residences in particular. Thus, when the museum opened in the Grande Galerie soon afterwards, as well as paintings there were already 124 objects of varied descriptions on view – marble and porphyry vases, clocks and porcelain, including the huge Sèvres vase in a mount by Thomire which is still on view in the rooms of the Department today.

The number of exhibits subsequently increased in a variety of different ways. The treasure of the Abbey of Saint-Denis, the finest church treasure in France under the *ancien régime*, which had already been raided in 1791 for the benefit of the Cabinet of Antiquities at the Bibliothèque Nationale, was brought to Paris in 1793 and there was a threat that it would be melted down, but the intervention of the Commission des Monuments resulted in some items being spared and transferred to the Louvre on 5 December 1793: the serpentine paten which may come from the Charles the Bald, the vases collected and mounted by Abbé Suger in the twelfth century, the silver-gilt Virgin donated to the abbey by Queen Jeanne d'Evreux, the regalia used at the coronations of the kings of France – Charles V's sceptre, the sword and spurs. These items, the incunabula of French goldsmithing, are among the glories of the Department's current collections.

Moreover, the Department of Objets d'Art can be seen as the successor to one of Europe's first museums. The Garde-Meuble de la Couronne (the administrative department responsible for furnishing royal palaces), which from 1774 was based in the premises on the Place de la Concorde now housing the Ministry of the Navy, had exhibition rooms that were open to the public a few days each year. These included the weapons room, part of the contents of which are now at the Musée de l'Armée, the furniture room, which contained the hangings illustrating the story of Deborah now held by the Department, and the jewel room with the Crown Jewels and the *pietre dure* vases collected by Louis XIV; there were also galleries of paintings and bronzes. In 1791 the Constituent Assembly published a partial inventory of these collections, expressing the wish that they should go to the Museum. Most of the *pietre dure* vases did in fact come to the Louvre in 1796. These vases, illustrating that branch of art from antique times until the seventeenth century, represent one of the most complete collections in the world. The bronzes from the Garde-Meuble, particularly rich in works by Giambologna, form the nucleus of the Department's collection of Renaissance bronzes. Another possible source for enhancing its collections was the decree issued on 1 Germinal, year II (21 March 1794) authorizing the Museum to take material from the repository of property confiscated from emigrants at the Hôtel de Nesle, but the

Joseph Auguste
The Jewel Room at the Louvre and the suite of Charles X Rooms,
c. 1835
Oil on canvas
100 x 81 cm
RF 3630

7

Louvre's collection of *objets d'art* benefited very little from this, only acquiring such things as the portrait in painted enamel of Anne de Montmorency, Constable of France. It was only a century later that furniture confiscated from emigrants came to the Louvre through the Garde-Meuble after having been used in the Imperial and royal palaces throughout the nineteenth century.

On the other hand, from 1794 onwards the Museum acquired many items as a result of Revolutionary and Imperial conquests. It had been envisaged from the outset that the collection would be enlarged through purchases: the helmet and shield of Charles IX were bought at auction in 1793.

The quality of this first disparate nucleus consisting of objects steeped in history and yet blazing a trail in the history of art was already extremely high. However, there was not enough interest in these objects for them to be assigned to a department of their own. When Vivant Denon became director of the Musée Central des Arts in 1802 – it was renamed Musée Napoléon in 1803 – the Museum's collections were divided into three sections: paintings, drawings, and antiquities. *Objets d'art* came under the last heading. The Department of Antiquities was entrusted to Ennio Quirino Visconti, and on his death in 1818 to Comte de Clarac.

A variety of factors combined to diminish the original collection. Sixteen items from the treasure of Saint-Denis were sold in 1798 at no profit to the museum. Napoleon requisitioned bronzes and *pietre dure* vases to decorate his palaces and some of these were subsequently lost. Works from other countries could be retained under the terms negotiated in 1814, but had to be returned to their country of origin after 1815.

This last loss was part of the reason why an active purchasing policy was pursued in the Restoration period. It affected *objets d'art*, which increased in number considerably thanks to the purchase of the Durand and Révoil collections. Edme-Antoine Durand (1768–1835) was a wealthy art-lover who had travelled widely in Italy where he discovered Greek and Roman antiquities, the field that interested him most. He sold his collection to the Louvre in 1825, no doubt in order to use the money to start again. As well as several thousand antiquities the inventory includes some 550 items illustrating Durand's interest in the medieval and Renaissance arts that employed firing techniques: *champlevé* enamels from the Meuse and Limoges, translucent enamels from the International Gothic period such as the two mirror valves belonging to Louis I of Anjou, Italian majolica, glazed earthenware ascribed to Bernard Palissy, painted enamels from the sixteenth century and stained glass. The "troubadour" painter Pierre Révoil (1776–1842) had passed through David's studio where he had made the acquaintance of Comte de Forbin who became Director of the Musées Royaux under the Restoration; this was helpful in ensuring that his collection was bought by the Louvre in 1828. There are 839 items listed in the inventory. Révoil was the first French collector to form a collection devoted exclusively to the Middle Ages and the Renaissance, the periods which provided inspiration for his paintings. He made purchases in every field (enamels, ivories, tapestries, furniture – the first to come into the Louvre) ranging from small items to masterpieces such as the Alpais ciborium. The Museum now had a coherent collection of *objets d'art* for the Middle Ages and the Renaissance exemplifying every technique; this was presented in what is now the Campana Gallery.

Louis-Philippe did not carry on this good work, but during his reign the Louvre was fortunate enough to receive the treasure of the Order of the Saint-Esprit (founded by Henri III) when it was abolished in 1830, the finest surviving group of Renaissance silverware in France.

When Clarac died in 1847 a change took place: Egyptian and Oriental Antiquities became independent and Greek and Roman Antiquities were entrusted to Comte (subsequently Marquis) de Laborde along with "modern" sculpture and *objets d'art*. Laborde was released from his duties in 1848 but returned to the Louvre in 1849 with responsibility for sculpture and *objets d'art* only; he resigned in 1854.

The Second Empire witnessed another spectacular expansion of the Louvre's collections of *objets d'art*, initially through the creation of the Musée des Souverains, a prestigious but short-lived venture. Wanting to provide his dynasty with a historical basis, on 15 February 1852 Napoleon III as prince-president issued a decree instituting this new section in the Louvre. The museum brought together mementoes of French sovereigns, from Childeric to Louis-Philippe, from the collections belonging to the Louvre, the Garde-Meuble, the Bibliothèque Nationale and the Musée d'Artillerie as well as gifts, generally modest in scale. It was housed in the first five rooms at the south end of the east wing of the Cour Carrée. Comte Horace de Viel-Castel, the famous writer of memoirs, was appointed curator of the museum; *objets d'art* were brought into it in 1854 and he was succeeded by Henry Barbet de Jouy in 1863.

Another two great collections came to the Louvre during this period, the Sauvageot collection and the Campana collection. As he had no private means Charles Sauvageot (1781–1860) pursued a double career as a customs official and a violinist at the Opéra in order to assemble a collection of medieval and – more particularly – Renaissance objects of varying importance, under the motto '*Dispersa coegi*'. He donated it to the museum in 1856 and was given lodgings in the Louvre where he was able to continue enjoying his collection until he died. The catalogue of this group of works (1861) has 1,424 entries including 96 pieces of glazed earthenware of the "Palissy school", which left the Louvre well provided in that field. Marchese Giampietro Campana di Cavelli, who was the director of the Monte di Pietà bank in Rome, collected Italian Primitives, antique ceramics and majolica with such unscrupulous passion that the Vatican ordered his arrest in 1857, seizing and selling his collection which was bought by Napoleon III in 1861. It was exhibited initially at the Palais de l'Industrie in the Champs-Elysées as the Musée Napoléon III, then given to the Louvre by a decree issued on 11 July 1862, making it one of the foremost museums in the world for majolica. Single important purchases were also made during the Second Empire, such as the ivory Virgin from the Sainte-Chapelle at Prince Soltykoff's sale in 1861.

The Department's first series of catalogues started to be published from the time of the Second Republic: the *Notice* for enamels was produced by Laborde in 1852–53 and followed by *Notices* for ivories, wooden items, faience, gems, glass and bronzes (1863–1874). The increased size and importance of the collection of *objets d'art* justified improving its presentation. In 1861 *pietre dure*, silverware and enamel were installed in wooden showcases gilded in Louis XIV style in the Galerie d'Apollon, where restoration work had been completed in 1851; the showcases had been specially made by the sculptor and *ébéniste* Gasc, from drawings by the architect Rossigneux, and some are still there. The rest of the collection was displayed on the first floor of the north wing of the Cour Carrée. It was decided to group objects by material in eight rooms which were inaugurated by the Emperor and Empress on 15 August 1863: an ivory room, a room for carved wood, terracotta, alabaster and sandstone (the Salle Sauvageot), a glass room, a room for objects made of iron, copper, pewter and bronze, a room of French faience, and three rooms for majolica.

When the Musée des Souverains was closed by decree on 8 May 1872 most of the objects it had exhibited were returned to the institutions from which they had come, or to their donors. The Louvre profited very little from this. The ministerial decree of 10 October 1871 ordained that sculpture from the Middle Ages, Renaissance and Modern period should be combined with *objets d'art* from the Middle Ages and Renaissance period under the aegis of Barbet de Jouy. He was succeeded by Edmond Saglio, from 1879 to 1893, when sculpture was separated from *objets d'art* yet again. From then on the collection of *objets d'art* was known as the Department of Objets d'Art from the Medieval, Renaissance and Modern Periods. Asiatic and Islamic arts, which had expanded greatly, were excluded from the collection in 1932. The direction of the Department was first entrusted to Emile Molinier who resigned in 1902.

Since 1870 the collections have increased in four different ways: transfers from the Garde-Meuble (now the Mobilier National), gifts, purchases and – since the law enacted on 31 December 1968 – dations. These additions which had previously related only to the Middle Ages and the Renaissance extended to modern times in two stages:

at the end of the nineteenth century to the seventeenth and eighteenth centuries, and in the third quarter of the twentieth century to the first half of the nineteenth centuries.

Items transferred from the Garde-Meuble form the basis of the current collection of furniture, bronzes, tapestries and carpets from the seventeenth and eighteenth centuries. A decision reached by the Commission de la Liste Civile et du Domaine Privé (Committee responsible for the Civil List and Private Property of the Emperor) on 12 September 1870, just a few days after the fall of the Second Empire, assigned furniture and objects from the Tuileries Palace and the Palace of Saint-Cloud to the Louvre: both buildings burnt down a short time later. The furniture included, in particular, works by Boulle which embellished the Galerie d'Apollon. The rest of it was scattered throughout the Museum.

It was another thirty years before *objets d'art* from the modern period were really integrated into the collections belonging to the Department of Objets d'Art. Molinier organized a retrospective exhibition of French art to coincide with the 1900 Exhibition, and the collections of the Garde-Meuble museum which had been established at the Garde-Meuble, 103 quai d'Orsay, in 1882 played a large part in it. When it was over Molinier managed to secure many works from the Garde-Meuble for the Louvre by means of the decree of 24 February 1901, and its museum then closed. The display of the seventeenth- and eighteenth-century collections in the five first-floor rooms at the north end of the west wing of the Cour Carrée was officially opened on 20 May 1901. Items continued to be transferred to the Louvre from the Mobilier National on an occasional basis, one of the most recent being Charles X's bed at the Tuileries in 1965.

The Department still also has some famous stones which used to belong to the royal collections; these are on show in the Galerie d'Apollon. The law of 10 December 1886 unfortunately ordained that the Crown Jewels should be sold, an event which took place at the Louvre from 12 to 23 May 1887. The "Régent" diamond, the "Côte-de-Bretagne" ruby and the reliquary brooch belonging to Empress Eugénie were among the most notable items that were preserved and assigned to the museum.

Gifts have made a considerable contribution to the growth of the Department's collections, whether involving whole collections such as the Sauvageot one or single items. Gifts of great collections serve as landmarks in the history of the Department in the late nineteenth century and the first half of the twentieth. Some were encyclopaedic in nature, while others were devoted to one period or one technique. One of the earliest and most outstanding was the collection of Adolphe Thiers (1797–1877); in his house on the Place Saint-Georges he had amassed a collection which set out to be "a summary of the arts of the universe". Madame Thiers (d. 1880) bequeathed it to the Louvre along with her own collection of porcelain, stipulating that all the objects should remain together. The Thiers collection goes beyond the Department's current parameters as it includes objects from Antiquity and from the Far East.

The collection bequeathed by Baronne Salomon de Rothschild in 1922 is also very varied in nature. It brought the Department its choicest examples of Venetian glass, many other French and Italian Renaissance items, such as the majolica plate bearing the arms of Isabella D'Este, and works from the eighteenth century.

The first collections concentrating on particular periods to come to the Department related only to the Middle Ages and the Renaissance. This applies to the Davillier, Adolphe de Rothschild and Arconati Visconti collections. Items bequeathed by Baron Charles Davillier (d. 1883) include the tapestry of the *Offering of the heart, Arion* by Riccio and five pieces of Medici porcelain. Baron Adolphe de Rothschild (d. 1900) bequeathed silverware intended for religious use, including the polyptych from the Abbey of Floreffe (13th century). The outstanding aspect of the collection donated in 1916 by Marchesa Arconati Visconti, who was advised by Molinier, is its French Renaissance furniture. Victor Martin Le Roy, the greatest French collector of the early twentieth century in the medieval field, made a gift of fourteen pieces of silverware. In 1919 Félix Doistau, an industrialist and a painter, made a gift of part of his collection, which further enhanced the medieval collection.

The first donations relating specifically to the eighteenth century came at the beginning of this century, after the seventeenth- and eighteenth-century rooms had been opened. Comte Isaac de Camondo (d. 1911) left all his collections to the Louvre: Impressionist paintings, Far Eastern art and eighteenth-century *objets d'art*. As it had been stipulated that his collection should not be broken up for fifty years, it was installed in eight rooms on the second floor of the Louvre between the Mollien staircase and the Grande Galerie. In his will Baron Basile de Schlichting (d. 1914), a Russian who had made his home in France, gave the curators of the Louvre permission to select anything they wanted from his collection of eighteenth-century furniture and objects. The monkey commode by Cressent was among the more notable items selected. The Schlichting collection was housed in the north gallery of the Flore wing.

Other generous benefactors made gifts of collections devoted to one technique. The earliest of these to come to the Department was that of Monsieur and Madame Philippe Lenoir, bequeathed to the Louvre in 1874; it forms the nucleus of the Louvre's collection of snuff-boxes. The collection of watches came into being solely through gifts: the collection of the clock-maker Paul Garnier, donated in 1916, and that of the clock-maker Jules-René Olivier, bequeathed by his sister in 1935, along with the watches in the bequest made by Madame Claudius Côte. The Department is indebted to the bequest of Théophile Giraudeau (d. 1892) for its examples of Rouen faience, and to that of Antonin Personnaz (d. 1936) for 43 examples of Hispano-Moresque faience.

There were fewer gifts of entire collections after World War II, as there were fewer great collectors, but they did continue. In 1958 Mademoiselle Elisabeth Mège bequeathed the collection of her father Charles Mège to the Louvre; this particular bequest benefited the medieval enamels and ivories section. These same fields were enriched in 1960 by the bequest of Madame Claudius Côte who divided the collection of her husband, an industrialist and scholar from Lyons, among quite a few museums. Monsieur René Grog, a Swiss industrialist, was one of the greatest collectors of eighteenth-century French objects in the post-war period. In 1973 he and his wife, Madame Carven, donated their superb collection, reserving the right of usufruct; the Louvre collections had nothing to compare with its Gobelins tapestries and furniture by Boulle, Joseph and Carlin. The Louvre had nothing representing the modern period in its collection of silverware, but this was remedied in the course of a few years thanks to two gifts. In 1946 Monsieur and Madame David David-Weill presented the finest pieces in their collection of silver, works by Thomas Germain in particular. Then in 1955, when the collection of the goldsmith Louis-Victor Puiforcat was about to be sold in Paris, Stavros Niarchos bought the finest pieces in it and gave them to the Louvre, reserving the right of usufruct. The famous golden goblet known as Anne of Austria's goblet was among these. Madame Nicolas Landau put the Louvre in immediate possession of an outstanding collection of scientific instruments when she presented her husband's collection to the museum in 1979.

A great many gifts of single objects chosen with discernment have served to strengthen various aspects of the Department's collections. Mention should be made of all the gifts made by the Société des Amis du Louvre (Association of Friends of the Louvre) founded in 1898; its first tribute to the Department was the gift of the tapestry of the *Last judgement* in 1901. Its continuing generosity has been confirmed by such gifts as the Meuse *armilla* (1934) or Empress Eugénie's pearl diadem (1992).

The Department has other friends and sometimes nowadays corporate patronage to thank for major works such as the chiffonnière with vernis Martin and Sèvres porcelain by B.V.R.B. (bequeathed by the antiquarian Francis Guérault in 1930), masterpieces in ivory such as *Nicodemus* (a gift from the children of Baron and Baronne Robert de Rothschild, 1947) and the Homberg Christ (a gift from Monsieur Guy Ladrière, 1984), Pierre Crozat's leather armchairs (a gift from Comte Robert-Henry de Caumont La Force, 1989), and the "grand salon" from the Château d'Abondant (donated by the L. Lafon Laboratory, 1989).

In 1966 the Empire and Restoration periods were given right of entry into the Department where they were represented by a few outstanding pieces of furniture. When the Musée d'Orsay was created, a time limit was placed on the chronological development of the Louvre: it stopped at 1850. The opening in 1986 of the Musée d'Orsay where a collection of *objets d'art* dating from 1850 and after were on view served to emphasize the Louvre's lack of objects dating from the first half of the nineteenth century. Generous patrons who are aware of this gap have already come forward to help enable the Department to illustrate this period at the same high level as those preceding it. The crystal toilet table of the Duchesse de Berry and the tapestry with the elephant, a masterpiece produced by the Aubusson factories during the reign of Louis-Philippe, have therefore come to embellish the Department's rooms thanks to Monsieur Claude Ott (1989) and Madame Simone Cino del Duca (1995).

Purchases still related only to objects from the medieval and Renaissance periods well after gifts from later periods had been received. Soon after the Third Republic was established one of the most outstanding purchases was that of the collection belonging to the painter Charles Timbal, including a wealth of Gothic ivories; it was bought in 1882 with a special credit approved by both chambers of Parliament. Emile Molinier subsequently bought a great many medieval objects of outstanding merit, such as the thirteenth-century ivory of the *Descent from the Cross* (1896). Fewer purchases were made in the inter-war period, although some excellent Renaissance bronzes such as the *Gnome with the snail* (1933) were bought then, as was one of the first eighteenth-century works to be purchased for the Department, the famous andirons made for the Palais-Royal bearing the signature of François-Thomas Germain (1935). After the war, Pierre Verlet and his successors still tried to buy any important works from the medieval and Renaissance periods that came on the market: the reliquary crown from the Dominican monastery at Liège (1947); the Limoges reliquary of St Antonin (1971); the arm reliquary of St Luke (1982); an Ottonian ivory panel of *Christ pointing to a child* (1993); the *Monkey* by Giambologna (1982). But Pierre Verlet also recognized the huge gaps in furniture, porcelain and silverware in the eighteenth-century collection, and made every effort to fill them. That is how the commode by Leleu originating from the Palais-Bourbon (1953), the pair of armoires by Cressent (1974), the seats by Heurtaut made for the drawing room of the Château de La Roche-Guyon (1975), and Marie Leczinska's lacquer commode from Fontainebleau (1988) came to be bought. In the field of Sèvres porcelain there were virtually no examples in the Department's collections of the spectacular but perplexing vases made by the Sèvres factory. A first purchase of eleven vases at the Harewood sale in 1965 was followed by many others. Where silverware is concerned, Marie Antoinette's "nécessaire", pieces originally ordered by Joseph I of Portugal, and pieces from the Duc de Penthièvre's service which had belonged to Louis-Philippe were bought to enhance the collection. It now became proper for purchases to relate to the nineteenth century too: the Wine Harvest Cup by Froment-Meurice (1984), and a pair of "Clodion" Sèvres vases which were a present from Louis XVIII to his brother (1991).

The lacquer bureau made by Carlin for Madame Victoire, a daughter of Louis XV, at the Château de Bellevue was the first item to come to the Department through dation. Since then there has been a steady stream of dations, bringing the Department important items of great value to the national heritage: a set of Gobelins tapestries illustrating the *Story of Don Quixote*, a silver service made by Robert-Joseph Auguste for George III, fine medieval works from the Martin Le Roy collection, and furniture decorated with Sèvres porcelain from the Rothschild collections, putting the Louvre at the forefront in a field that had hitherto been the preserve of British and American museums.

Several series of catalogues have been devoted to studying the collections: scholarly catalogues instigated by Molinier, concise catalogues which appeared between 1910 and 1920, and contemporary catalogues, some of which have been published while others are in preparation.

There were so many additions to the collections at the end of the nineteenth century and the beginning of the twentieth that it became essential to consider reorganizing the way they were presented. In the inter-war period the medieval and Renaissance collections were dispersed between the Galerie d'Apollon and the north wing of the Cour Carrée where they had been since the Second Empire, as well as occupying part of the east wing. The seventeenth- and eighteenth-century collections were also fragmented since – as we have seen – it was not possible for the Camondo and Schlichting bequests to be integrated into the rest of the collection. The reorganization of the medieval and Renaissance collections was started in 1935 thanks to Henri Verne, director of the Musées Nationaux. The new display, regrouping the collections in the whole of the east wing, was opened officially on 24 June 1938. The Department occupied seven rooms, some of which had formerly been used for the Musée des Souverains. Wood panelling had been installed in the first three at the time of the Restoration and they seemed to form a grand antechamber to the next four in which objects were now displayed chronologically rather than by technique: two rooms were devoted to the Middle Ages, and two to the Renaissance. The first Renaissance room in the Pavillon Saint-Germain-l'Auxerrois contained bronzes and silverware. The second had been designed to enable the twelve large tapestries representing *The hunts of Maximilian* – brought together for the first time – to be exhibited, along with ceramics and painted enamels. The showcases along the walls and in the centre, made of medal-coloured patinated copper, were illuminated by electric lighting, an innovation for the Louvre, and supported on pedestals made of natural wood or, in some cases, on old pieces of furniture from the collection of chests and tables. The showcases in the two medieval rooms were replaced by more modern ones with metal bases in 1981. The 1938 presentation was a remarkable step forward, but because of a shortage of space too few objects were exhibited on their own. The tapestries were hung too high, above the showcases. The reorganization of the Modern Period collections had also been under consideration before the war, and it was implemented gradually after the war in the north and west wings of the Cour Carrée by Pierre Verlet; the rooms were opened between 1962 and 1966.

Even so the presentation of the collections was becoming increasingly crowded by the end of the 1970s. The Department was therefore delighted to hear in 1981 that the area of the Louvre occupied by the Ministry of Finance was to be assigned to the Museum. The redeployment of its collections suggested to the Department by the Etablissement Public du Grand Louvre in 1984 was met with the same satisfaction. The Department has lost the east wing of the Cour Carrée, but gained the whole of the first floor of the former Ministry, so taking over the famous apartments furnished for the Ministry of State between 1856 and 1861 in the reign of Napoleon III, which have retained their original furnishings. With Jean-Michel Wilmotte's assistance the additional space has enabled the Department on the one hand to redeploy its medieval and Renaissance collections which are now displayed chronologically, and on the other to exhibit its Empire collections near the Napoleon III apartments. It has at last become possible to bring some works which – through lack of space, wall space in particular – had never been displayed (several stained-glass windows) or not for a very long time (the Deborah hangings, various tapestries) out of the reserves. Spaces were created specially to match the dimensions of some groups of works, such as the two large galleries for the tapestries illustrating *The hunts of Maximilian* and the *Story of Scipio*, a room for the Venetian Renaissance ceiling acquired through the bequest of Baron Adolphe de Rothschild, a room devoted to the chapel of the Order of the Saint-Esprit, another to housing a reconstruction of Madame Récamier's bedroom: her bed was given to the Department by the Amis du Louvre in 1991. Two rooms in the Napoleon III apartments which no longer have their furnishings have been used for the Thiers collection. All the new rooms were officially opened on 18 November 1993 to coincide with the bicentenary of the Museum.

The Department still has to reorganize the seventeenth- and eighteenth-century rooms in their present site and complete the display of the nineteenth-century, Restoration and Louis-Philippe collections. These are to be housed after the Empire rooms in an area that is as yet unoccupied.

Late Antiquity
and the early Middle Ages

In the third AD century a series of political, military, economic and social crises brought about very profound changes in Roman society in the late Empire. One of the crucial factors was certainly the rapid spread of Christianity in the second and third centuries, and the growing assurance of the Church in the course of the fourth century. Christianity was tolerated by Constantine from 313–314 and became the official religion of Rome on the death of Theodosius in 395. As Rome turned its back on pagan deities the first Christian art appeared on the scene. The Church triumphant then erected a new kind of temple more suited to the requirements of its liturgy. Taking over antique figurative traditions, it produced countless Christian images in mosaic, marble and ivory. On the panel carved in low relief depicting the *Miracles of Christ*, produced in Rome c. 400 and subsequently sawn in three, the short canon, the youthful faces and the classic drapery of the protagonists typify an artistic tradition inherited from antiquity.

Germanic tribes, probably driven westwards by the Huns, were threatening Rome from beyond the Rhine and the Danube on the frontier of the Empire which was guarded by the legions. However, there was already a great deal of contact between Rome and the barbarians, although everything seemed to argue against it; there were even barbarians serving the Empire. Stilicho, who had a Vandal father and a Roman mother, held the highest State offices shortly before 400; he was in overall command of the Roman armies and married Serena, the emperor's niece. Their daughter Maria married the young Emperor Honorius at Milan in 398. Empress Maria's bulla, a tiny jewel found in her grave at St Peter's in Rome in 1544, unites their names on the two sard cameos set in a gold mounting embellished with emeralds and rubies; the letters of their names form a chrism.

A few years later the great Germanic invasions starting in 406 brought about the collapse of the Western Roman Empire; it finally disappeared in 476. But the barbarians had to come to terms with the Church which was the only remaining haven of Roman civilization. In Gaul Clovis (481–511), the chief of the Salian Franks, succeeded in asserting his authority by means of his conversion to Christianity, becoming the first king in the Merovingian dynasty. Antique traditions and barbarian customs tended to become merged and the survival of the Roman heritage, basically Christian but very influenced by barbarian trends, was to leave its mark on Merovingian civilization (6th–8th century). This also applied to the other barbarian kingdoms that became established in the West from the fifth century on.

The contents of Merovingian tombs often help give us a better idea of their civilization. One of the finest examples was found in 1958, when excavations were carried out at the abbey church of Saint-Denis in a group of royal and princely tombs. It consists of a number of woman's jewels made of gold and *cloisonné* garnets, and silver garter and shoe ornaments; these have been identified as belonging to Queen Arégonde, the wife of Clotaire I (d. 558),

Equestrian statuette: Charlemagne or Charles the Bald
Carolingian art, 9th century
Bronze. Height 23.5 cm
Provenance, treasury of Metz cathedral
OA 8260

by means of the monogram on the golden sigillary ring, a custom that is Roman in origin. On the other hand the absence of human figures, except for the outline of a head sketched on the large buckle-plate and, more particularly, the perfection of the goldsmithing techniques used are derived from decorative concepts peculiar to the barbarian arts, especially the cloisonné technique applied to gold and silver work where thin plates of table-cut garnet are set in fine bands of gold that form a geometric pattern.

The conquest of Italy and the unification of the Christian West under Charlemagne at the end of the eighth century rekindled the idea of a universal empire, leading to Charlemagne being crowned emperor in Rome in 800. Thus a deliberate intention to revive Constantine's empire characterized the "Carolingian Renaissance". The work which may best symbolize this tendency is the bronze statuette in the Louvre showing Charlemagne or his grandson Charles the Bald on horseback. This statue – the only Carolingian work in the round to have survived to our day – draws its inspiration from antique equestrian statues, such as the one of Marcus Aurelius on the Capitol; it probably even reuses a horse made in the Late Empire period. The move back to antique models is just as perceptible in carving on ivory. The two panels from the binding of a psalter which Charlemagne commissioned from the scribe Dagulf as a gift for Pope Hadrian I (d. 795) carry on the art of narrative bas-relief with tremendous skill: the classical style and youthful faces of the protagonists in the scenes in which David composes the Psalms (left panel) and St Jerome translates them (right panel) are in fact reminiscent of Roman ivories dating from about 400, such as the panel depicting the *Miracles of Christ*.

But Carolingian Renaissance art undoubtedly achieved its most perfect expression in the reign of Charles the Bald (840–877), as several masterpieces in the Louvre associated with his activities as a patron attest. The serpentine paten inlaid with fish made of gold, a work dating from the antique period, was provided with a superb mount made of gold, precious stones and *cloisonné* garnets by a goldsmith at the court of Charles the Bald; the king presented it and a chalice to the Abbey of Saint-Denis. Only the antique cup of the chalice is still in existence, the famous Cup of the Ptolemies at the Bibliothèque Nationale. The ivory panel depicting the episode from the Bible in which Abner and Joab meet beside the lake at Gibeon also comes from the treasure of Saint-Denis; it must have adorned one of the many manuscripts which Charles the Bald gave to the abbey and is among the finest pieces made by the king's workshops, as is the panel known as the panel of "earthly Paradise". This in fact represents the different orders of Creation, after Isidore of Seville's *Etymologiae*, with man at their head; it is carved on the back of a consular ivory dating from late Antiquity and was produced by the same workshop that is credited with the carvings on the ivory throne at St Peter's in Rome.

However, the Carolingian Renaissance was as short-lived as it was brilliant. Disputes about the succession setting Charlemagne's descendants at odds with one another and new invasions, Norman to the north and west, Hungarian to the east, put an end to Carolingian ambitions. From the beginning of the tenth century the empire disappeared and a new order was worked out in the West which gave rise to Romanesque art.

Empress Maria's bulla
Milan (?), between 398
and 407
Agate cameos, gold, emeralds, rubies
Diameter 1.8 cm
Anonymous gift, 1951
OA 9523

Miracles of Christ
Side panel of a five-panel diptych
Rome, beginning of 5th century
Ivory. Height 19.7 cm; width 7.8 cm
Acquired in 1926
OA 7876-7878

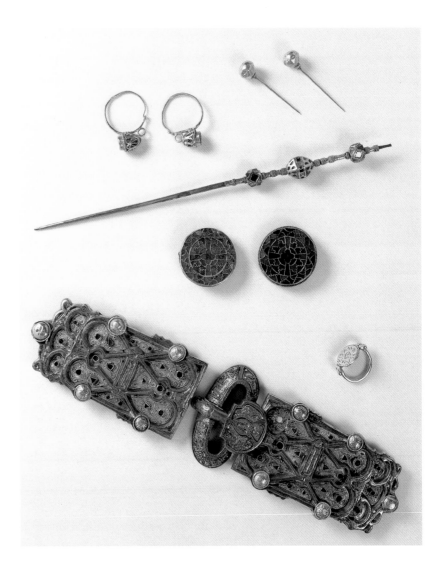

*Jewels belonging to
Queen Arégonde*
Merovingian Gaul, 6th century
Gold, cloisonné garnets, blue glass,
filigree, silver, nielli
Found in 1958 during excavations
at the basilica of Saint-Denis

During Charlemagne's reign the Carolingian Renaissance first manifested itself in the court workshops, with most artists such as Dagulf – the Louvre owns the two ivories that formed the binding of the Psalter he created – being grouped round the sovereign. However those close to the emperor were also endowed with powerful bishoprics or rich abbeys which in turn became centres of creative activity. Thus, in the reign of Charles the Bald several workshops vied with one another to serve the king, including that at Saint-Denis, the abbey which Charles the Bald had elected as his burial-place, where several of the most outstanding pieces commissioned by him originated.

Panel known as
"Earthly paradise"
France, c. 860-870
Ivory. Height 35.8 cm; width 11.5 cm
Acquired in 1863
OA 9064

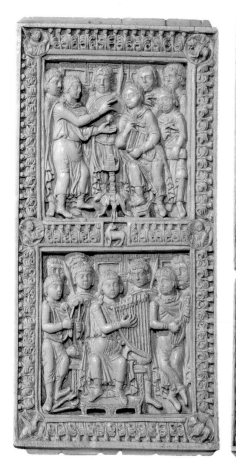

Binding of Dagulf's Psalter:
David, St Jerome
Charlemagne's palace workshop,
before 795
Ivory. Height 16.8 cm;
width of each panel 8.1 cm
Old collection
MR 370-371

Serpentine paten
Stone: 1st century BC or AD,
and (fishes, made of incrusted
gold) late Empire;
mount: second half of 9th century,
court of Charles the Bald
Serpentine, gold, precious stones, pearls
Diameter 17 cm
Provenance, treasure of Saint-Denis
MR 415

Panel from binding:
Meeting of Abner and Joab
beside the lake of Gibeon
Court of Charles the Bald,
c. 870-875
Ivory. Height 15.4 cm; width 8.2 cm
Provenance, treasury of Saint-Denis
MR 374

ΤΩΣ ΕΥΠΡΕΠΗΣ ΤΑΙΣ ΓΥΝΑΙΞΙΝ Ο ΑΓΓΕΛΟΣ

ΕΙΧΕ
ΔΕ ΑΙ ΤΑΣ
ΤΡΟ
ΜΟΣ ΚΑΙ
ΕΚΨΑΣΙΣ

ΔΕΥΤΕ ΙΔΕΤΟΝ ΤΟΠΟΝ
ΟΠΟΥ ΕΚΕΙΤΟ Ο ΚΣ

Ο
ΤΑ
ΦΟΣ
ΤΟΥ
ΚΥ

ΚΑΙ ΟΙ
ΦΥΛΑΣ
ΣΟΝΤΕΣ
ΑΠΕΝΕ
ΚΡΩΘΗ
ΣΑΝ

ΕΜ
ΦΥ
ΤΩ
ΣΥ
Μ
ΒΟ
ΛΑ
ΑΥ
ΚΑ
ΘΑ
ΡΟ
ΤΗ
ΤΟ
ΤΗ
ΥΡ
ΦΗ
ΤΕ
ΜΗ
ΝΥ
ШΤ
ΟΦ
ΕΠ

Η
ΝΥ
ΕΜ
ΠΕ
ΦΑ
ΝΗ
ΚΑΙ
ΗΛ
ΑΥ
ΓΗ
ΙΦ
ΕΡ
Ш
ΝΗ
Σ

ΑΠΑΣΕΩΣ ΚΡΑΖΙШ   ΓΕΡΘΕΝ Ο ΚΣ

Byzantium

The Western Roman Empire disappeared during the fifth century, but the Eastern Roman or Byzantine Empire survived for almost another thousand years until Constantinople, the capital of the empire, fell to the Turks in 1453. Constantine, who is regarded as the first Christian emperor, had founded the city on the shores of the Bosphorus in 330. It presided over a group of formerly Roman territories in the eastern part of the Mediterranean Basin which linguistically and culturally were predominantly Greek. Thus Byzantium was the heir to both Rome and the East, to Hellenism and Christianity.

Once the difficulties associated with the collapse of the Western Empire had been overcome, Byzantium had a first period of eminence in the 6th century in the reign of Justinian (526–561). The reconquest of Italy, where the mosaics in San Vitale in Ravenna immortalise the glory of Justinian and Theodora, was matched by the construction of St Sophia in Constantinople: its huge dome remained unsurpassed for a very long time. But nothing better reflects the splendour and luxury of the works produced in the Imperial circle than the "Barberini ivory" depicting the triumph of an emperor, possibly Justinian himself. Vanquished nations are bringing their tributes to him in the presence of a general carrying a statuette of victory, with Christ appearing above the emperor in a mandorla supported by two angels: a supreme image of the theocratic concept of Imperial power which Byzantium supported to the very end.

A new danger appeared at the beginning of the seventh century, however, almost bringing about the empire's downfall. Within a few years Islam had wrested Egypt and Syria from Byzantium and reached the very walls of Constantinople to threaten its survival. The icons to which the people turned in their superstition were powerless against the Arab armies. To strengthen the state the emperors and the Church tried to reform religion and forcibly repress the cult of icons. Iconoclasm became official Byzantine policy in 726 and lasted for more than a century until religious orthodoxy and the cult of images were solemnly reinstated in 843.

The advent of the Macedonian dynasty (863–1056) immediately after the iconoclastic crisis ushered in Byzantium's second golden age. From the late ninth century a strong spirit of intellectual and artistic rebirth – the intellectual fervour that had stirred the opposing parties during the iconoclastic crisis had prepared the ground for this – made itself felt in Constantinople within the confined circles of the court and the Church, reaching its height in the tenth century before becoming more widely disseminated under the Comnenus dynasty (1081–1185). The move back to antique models can be seen particularly in the few secular works which have survived, such as the ivory caskets decorated with mythological scenes intended for the enjoyment of a cultured élite, where putti parody the heroes and divinities of pagan Antiquity in quite a humorous way. Their lively style, which is described as

Panel from the reliquary of the Stone from Christ's sepulchre: the Holy Women greeted by the angel at the tomb of Christ
Constantinople, 12th century (second half?)
Silver-gilt on wooden core
Height 42.6 cm; width 31 cm
Provenance, treasury of the Sainte-Chapelle
MR 348

"pictural", is obviously inspired by Hellenistic works. Although from 843 Byzantine religious art was firmly encoded, considered as a whole it too was deeply influenced by antique models, as the classical nobility and feeling for volume in the finest tenth-century Constantinople ivories show: the "Harbaville" triptych for instance, the product of an Imperial workshop which was also responsible for the famous panel in the Cabinet of Medals depicting Romanos II (945–963) and his first wife.

During the eleventh century and even more the twelfth the classicism acquired through the legacy of the Macedonian Renaissance was sometimes modified by a search for new decorative means, as shown by the delicate gold encrustations on the lapis lazuli icon from the Saint-Denis treasure, or the small coloured ornaments placed at intervals on St Demetrius's garments on the gold and *cloisonné* enamel medallion from the frame of an icon; the sophistication of the medallion is reminiscent of the enamels on the *Pala d'Oro* in Venice. It was still in the Comnenus period, probably in the second half of the twelfth century, that the silver-gilt panel with the Holy Women greeting the angel on the morning of the Resurrection was made. This panel was part of a reliquary of the Stone from Christ's sepulchre which in turn was one of a group of reliquaries relating to the Passion of Christ (the Crown of Thorns, the Holy Lance, the True Cross...) subsequently acquired by St Louis for the Sainte-Chapelle in Paris. The supreme elegance of the angel, the subtlety of the modelling and the studied gestures almost verging on Mannerism make it easy for us to understand the fascination Byzantine art exerted over the medieval West.

In 1204 the Fourth Crusade, which should like the others have been directed towards Jerusalem, altered course and attacked Constantinople which was captured and pillaged, with the Crusaders sharing out the remains of the Empire. The treasures of Byzantium were then taken to the West. This probably explains how the reliquary with sliding panels containing the True Cross came to France; when it was given to Jaucourt church in the Aube in the fourteenth century it was fitted with a Gothic mount in the shape of two angels exalting the relic.

Yet again Byzantium rose from its ashes when Michael Paleologus wrested Constantinople back from the westerners and revived the empire. In spite of being partially dismembered by the westerners, besieged by the Turks and soon virtually reduced to a city state, Byzantium experienced a last renaissance under Paleologi rule (1261–1453), especially in the pictorial field, reflected not only in icons but also in frescoes and mosaics. The *Transfiguration* in the Louvre, a portable mosaic icon made c. 1200 or early in the thirteenth century, is a token of the start of this final Byzantine renaissance. It still adheres to a kind of classicism but the search for expressiveness that typifies Paleologi art is already in evidence.

Five-part panel known as the "Barberini ivory":
Emperor in triumph
Constantinople, first half of 6th century
Ivory, remains of encrustations. Height 34.2 cm; width 26.8 cm
Discovered in Provence in 17th century
Acquired in 1899
OA 9063

Ewer
Byzantium. 7th century (?)
Sard. Height 17.8 cm
Formerly collection of Louis XIV
MR 116

"Harbaville" triptych:
Deësis and saints
Constantinople,
mid-10th century
Ivory, traces of gilding and painting
Height 24 cm; width (open) 28 cm
Acquired in 1891
OA 3247

Medallion: St Demetrius
Constantinople, end of 11th
or beginning of 12th century
Gold, repoussé cloisonné enamel on gold
Diameter 8 cm
From the frame of the icon of the Archangel
Gabriel from Djoumati monastery (Georgia)
J. Pierpont-Morgan gift, 1911
OA 6457

*Panel from a casket with a mythological
decoration : putti at play*
Constantinople, second half or end of 10th century
Detail
Ivory. Width 28.2 cm; height 4.8 cm
Acquired in 1991
OA 11329

Icon: The Transfiguration
Constantinople, c. 1200
or beginning of 13th century
Mosaic of gilt copper, marble, lapis lazuli and
glass on wax
Height 52 cm; width 35 cm
Acquired in 1852
ML 145

Lapis lazuli icon
Constantinople,
first half of 12th century
Lapis lazuli encrusted with gold,
silver-gilt, filigree,
precious stones, pearl
Height 10 cm
Former treasure of Saint-Denis
MR 95

Reliquary of the True Cross
Byzantium, 12th–13th century, and Champagne
(angels and base) c. 1320–1340
Silver-gilt on wooden core, silver-gilt (angels),
gilt copper (base)
Overall height 25 cm; width 38 cm
Provenance, Jaucourt church (Aube)
Acquired in 1915
OA 6749

The Middle Ages in the West

The political fragmentation which resulted from the disappearance of the Carolingian Empire partly explains the geographical diversity of Romanesque art (10th–12th centuries). In the east of Europe, however, Otto I breathed new life into the imperial concept by founding the Holy Roman Germanic Empire in 962; while elsewhere in Europe the year 1000 saw the emergence of the first forms of Romanesque art, Ottonian art was characterized by its obsession with Carolingian models. This is illustrated by the book-binding casket from Maastricht; its sumptuousness and the gold-smithing techniques employed are faithful to the very essence of Carolingian art. Yet sometimes a monumental character does anticipate Romanesque art, as on the openwork ivory panel depicting Christ pointing to a child from a group of works presented to Magdeburg cathedral by Otto I in 968. But until the end of the twelfth century the memory of Carolingian art and the weight of imperial traditions were very much alive in the art of the Holy Roman Empire; for instance, they are very visible in the style and iconography of the reliquary casket of Charlemagne's arm. Even so, from the mid-twelfth century they did not prevent more Romanesque forms from maturing along with the general rise in popularity of champlevé enamel on gilt copper. Thus in the Meuse regions a form of Romanesque art with classical overtones developed in the wake of the patronage of Wibald de Stavelot (1130–1158), as illustrated by the fine plaque with the centaur in the Louvre, as well as elsewhere, in Lower Saxony for instance, with the enamelled reliquary of the St Henry (Emperor Henry II) from Hildesheim.

In other regions Romanesque art flourished earlier, characterized by powerful stylization, a general subordination of the figures to the constraints of the frame, and an unfaltering spirit of invention drawing on every possible source. In southern Italy from the end of the eleventh century ivory-workers' workshops mixed antique references and Byzantine and Islamic influences to create amazing chess pieces, hunting-horns or such notable assemblages as the paliotto from Salerno cathedral, the source of the panel with Cain and Abel in the Louvre. Champlevé enamel on copper started to appear from the beginning of the twelfth century in Conques during Boniface's period as abbot, later developing fully in Limoges with such attractive works as the reliquary of St Martial with a vermiculate ground and continuing into the very early thirteenth century with the famous ciborium made by the master Alpais. In the Ile-de-France at Saint-Denis Abbé Suger (1122–1151) called on the finest artists of the day to produce some of the most splendid examples of Romanesque art, such as the amazing ewer in the shape of an eagle inspired by antique or Byzantine models; yet the accurate treatment of the plumage reveals a move towards naturalism which had not been seen before.

At Saint-Denis in the mid-twelfth century architecture and sculpture were in fact gradually moving away from Romanesque forms towards the beginnings

Alpais ciborium
Limoges, c. 1200
Gilt copper,
champlevé enamel.
Height 30 cm
Probable provenance,
tomb of
Bertrand de Malsang
(d. 1316),
abbot of Montmajour
Formerly Révoil collection
Acquired in 1828
MRR 98

of Gothic art. But painting and the luxury crafts made virtually no contribution to the general renewal before the 1180s, when a special style made its appearance in the Rhine and Meuse areas and northern France, centred on the goldsmith Nicolas de Verdun. The shoulder-piece in the Louvre depicting the Resurrection is an accomplished precursor of this "*style 1200*" which spread throughout Europe; it was characterized by antique-influenced drapery, freedom of movement and more natural attitudes, as on the stained-glass window of St Nicasius and St Eutropia originating from Soissons or the arched panel of Limoges enamel with St Matthew.

In the mid-thirteenth century in the reign of St Louis the workshops in Paris developed a new style. The ivory Virgin from the Sainte-Chapelle is one of its finest examples: the arched, twisting silhouette, the drapery with its multitude of sharp and fluted folds and the delicate triangular face with its long almond-shaped eyes are all distinctive feature of this style, which also occurs on the fine ivory statuettes in the group representing the *Descent from the Cross*. A school soon formed following this style, as the large silver-gilt polyptych which belonged to the Abbey of Floreffe demonstrates – there is some dispute as to whether it was made in Paris or the Meuse area. This new style marks the beginning of the refinements that characterized courtly Parisian art at the end of the thirteenth century and in the fourteenth: the drapery became more graphic, the silhouettes more sinuous and the modelling softer, both on works in ivory and silverware, as in the reliquary Virgin presented to the Saint-Denis treasury by Queen Jeanne d'Evreux in 1339. Technical perfection and sinuous fluidity of form reached their peak in the reign of Charles V (1364–1380), as is illustrated at the Louvre by the large ivory quatrefoil diptych, Charles V's gold sceptre or the mirror valves of enamelled gold made for Charles's brother Louis I of Anjou. Parisian elegance was exported throughout the fourteenth century, to Naples in the form of the arm reliquary of St Luke c. 1336–1338, or to England in the form of the thin ivory panel belonging to John Grandisson, Bishop of Exeter, c. 1350–1360, to such an extent that around 1400 the same "International" Gothic style was current throughout Europe. The dreamy, aristocratic idealism of the tapestry representing the *Offering of the heart* or the sumptuousness of the reliquary from the treasure of the Saint-Esprit embody the spirit of this style, while the small statue of the kneeling prophet from the base of the reliquary of St Germanus at Saint-Germain-des-Prés which conjures up the art of both Sluter and Ghiberti as a young man demonstrates its ambiguities.

From the beginning of the fifteenth century the rise of the Renaissance tends to overshadow the last achievements of medieval art, attractive as they are. Even in Florence majolica decoration long remained faithful to the medieval spirit, which also lingered on in Spain in the form of ceramics that are described as Hispano-Moresque. But while the Flamboyant style was getting out of hand in northern Europe, French art was characterized by a certain moderation, as demonstrated by the reliquary angels of Anne de Bretagne and – in particular – the self-portrait in the form of an enamel medallion thought up by the painter Jean Fouquet to sign the Melun diptych commissioned by Etienne Chevalier shortly after 1451. There are already premonitions of the concerns that would preoccupy the Renaissance period.

Panel: Christ pointing to a child
Court of Otto I, c. 968
Openwork ivory.
Height 12.5 cm; width 11.5 cm
Provenance, Magdeburg cathedral
Acquired in 1993
OA 11372

Bookbinding casket: the Crucifixion and the symbols of the Evangelists
Ottonian art, second quarter of 11th century
Gold, *cloisonné* enamels on gold, precious stones, filigree and nielli on wooden core. Height 32.2 cm
Acquired in 1795
MR 349

Reliquary of St Henry
Hildesheim (Lower Saxony), c. 1170
Gilt copper, champlevé enamel,
rock crystal and silver on wooden core
Height 23.6 cm
Provenance, St Michael's church, Hildesheim
Acquired in 1857
OA 49

Plaque: centaur
Meuse, c. 1160–1170
Gilt copper, champlevé enamel
Height 10 cm
V. Martin Le Roy gift, 1914
OA 8097

Reliquary of
Charlemagne's arm
Liège, c. 1165–1170
Champlevé enamel on copper,
silver-gilt on wooden core
Length 54 cm; height 13.6 cm
Provenance, Aix-la-Chapelle (Aachen) treasure
MR 347

Formal bracelet (armilla):
the Resurrection
Meuse, c. 1170–1175
Gilt copper, champlevé enamels
Height 11.3 cm; length 14.7 cm
Probable provenance,
tomb of Prince André Bogolowski at Vladimir
Gift of the Amis du Louvre, 1934
OA 8261

Medallion decorated
with a fantastic animal
Conques (?), c. 1107–1119
Gilt copper, champlevé enamel. Diameter 8 cm
From a casket commissioned for
the Conques treasury by Abbé Boniface
Gift of a group of friends of Victor Gay, 1909
OA 6280

Oliphant (hunting-horn)
Southern Italy, 11th–12th century
Ivory. Length 48 cm
Formerly Révoil Collection
Acquired in 1828
MRR 430

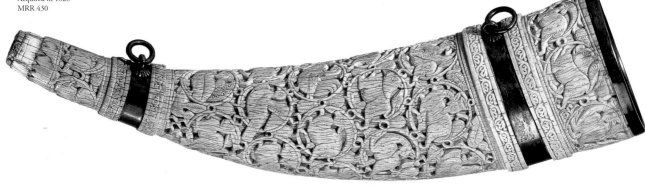

Panel:
Sacrifice of Cain
and Abel,
Abel's murder and
condemnation of Cain
Amalfi or Salerno, c. 1080
Ivory. Width 22.2 cm; height 0.9 cm
Acquired in 1898
OA 4052

Abbé Suger's eagle
Egypt or Imperial Rome
(porphyry vase)
Saint-Denis before 1147 (mount)
Porphyry, silver-gilt, niello
Height 43.1 cm; width 27 cm
Provenance, treasury of Saint-Denis
MR 422

Sword used at the coronation of
the kings of France, and sheath
Ile de France, 10th–11th century (pommel);
9th–10th and 12th centuries (cross bar); tang, Gothic; blade, modern;
Ile de France, end of 13th to beginning of 14th century (sheath)
Gold, silver-gilt and precious stones
Maximum height, 83.8 cm; width 22.6 cm
Provenance, treasury of Saint-Denis
MS 84

Arched panel: St Matthew
Limoges, c. 1220–1230
Gilt copper, champlevé enamel,
applied figure en demi ronde bosse
Height 28.4 cm
Formerly Durand collection
Acquired in 1825
MR 2650

Reliquary of St Francis of Assisi
Limoges, c. 1230
Gilt copper, champlevé enamel, glass beads,
on wooden core
Height 35.5 cm
Acquired in 1899
OA 4083

Reliquary of St Martial
Limoges, c. 1170–1180
Champlevé enamel on copper,
vermiculate ground
Height 12 cm; width 16 cm
V. Martin Le Roy gift, 1914
OA 8101

The luxury arts were also affected by the rise in popularity of monumental statuary in the thirteenth century, as evidenced by the ivory Virgin from the Sainte-Chapelle, carved in the round, which adopts and expands on the elegant style of the statues made for the apostolic college of the Sainte-Chapelle. But architecture in its turn contributed to the emergence of new forms; thus the silver polyptych originating from Floreffe is in the form of a small Gothic monument with a dais at the foot, decorative crockets and turrets at the top, the central panel enclosing two angels supporting a reliquary cross while the statuettes in the wings relate to episodes from the Passion. The ivory statuettes in the group portraying the *Descent from the Cross* were no doubt also formerly contained in an aedicule in the form of a tabernacle.

Virgin with Child from the Sainte-Chapelle
Paris, c. 1250–1260, before 1279
Ivory, traces of polychromy. Height 41 cm
Provenance, treasury of the Sainte-Chapelle
Acquired in 1861
OA 57

Scenes from the martyrdom of St Nicasius and St Eutropia
Northern France, beginning of 13th century
Detail of a stained glass window
Height 280 cm; width 154 cm
Provenance, Soissons
Acquired in 1905 and Mme O. Homberg gift, 1907
OA 6006 and 6119

*Reliquary polyptych of
the True Cross*
Meuse or northern France,
after 1254
Silver-gilt, gilt copper, nielli,
precious stones
Height 79 cm;
width when open 92 cm
Made for the Abbey of
Floreffe (Belgian Ardennes)
Baron A. de Rothschild bequest,
1901
OA 5552

*Group: Descent from
the Cross*
Paris, c. 1260–1280
Ivory, traces of polychromy
Maximum height 29 cm
Acquired in 1896 and gift of the
children of Baron and
Baronne de Rothschild, 1947
OA 3935 and 9443

Valve of a hinged mirror: chess game
Paris, c. 1300
Ivory, diameter 12 cm
C. Sauvageot gift, 1856
OA 117

Jeanne d'Evreux's *Virgin* is a crucial work in the development of Marian statuary: the twisting silhouette, the transversal apron-like draping of the cloak with the folds falling in scrolls at the sides, and the tenderness of the Child's hand movement can in fact be seen on many stone or marble statues of the Virgin with Child dating from the first half of the fourteenth century. (The reliquary fleur-de-lis held in her right hand used to contain some of the Virgin's milk, part of her veil and some of her hair.) The base which is embellished with plaques of translucent enamel worked in basse-taille on silver, representing scenes from the life of Christ, is one of the earliest dated Parisian examples of a technique that emerged at the end of the thirteenth century in Italy and spread throughout Europe during the fourteenth.

Reliquary statuette: Virgin and Child
of Jeanne d'Evreux
Paris, between 1324 and 1339
Silver-gilt, beaded gold, precious stones, translucent basse-taille enamels
Height 68 cm
Presented in 1339 to the treasury of Saint-Denis by Queen Jeanne d'Evreux,
widow of Charles IV "the Fair" (1324–1328)
MR 342

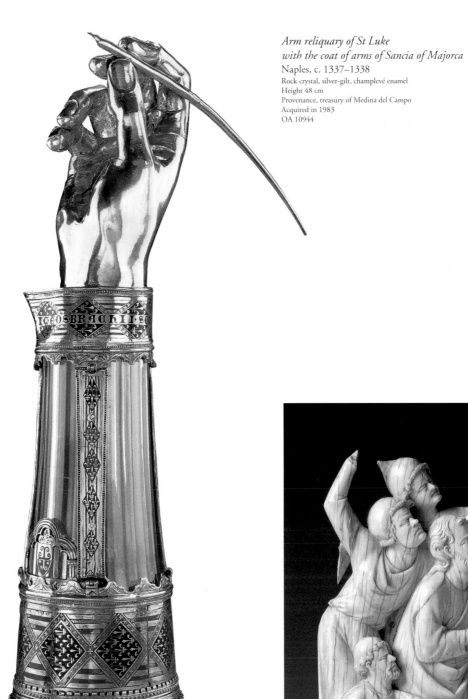

*Arm reliquary of St Luke
with the coat of arms of Sancia of Majorca*
Naples, c. 1337–1338
Rock crystal, silver-gilt, champlevé enamel
Height 48 cm
Provenance, treasury of Medina del Campo
Acquired in 1983
OA 10944

*Applied group:
Christ's arrest*
Paris, c. 1320-1330
Ivory. Height 18.6 cm
E. Mège bequest, 1958
OA 9961

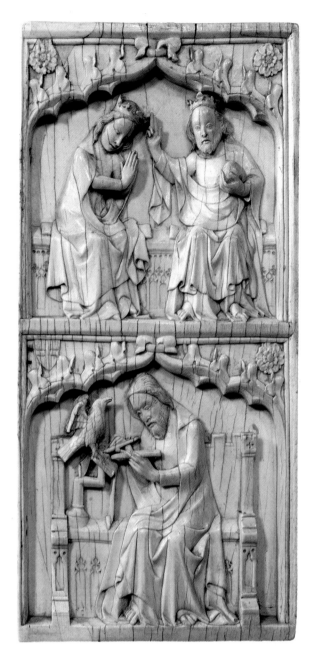

Panel: Coronation of the Virgin;
St John the Evangelist
England, before 1358
Ivory. Height 24 cm
Provenance, John Grandisson, Bishop of Exeter
C. Sauvageot gift, 1856
OA 105

The active role of King Charles V and his brothers as patrons of the arts partly explains the importance of Paris at the end of the fourteenth century, when artists from a number of different countries contributed towards elaborating the International Gothic style which became prevalent at all the courts of Europe. Paris, in fact, witnessed the emergence of one of the most magnificent goldsmithing techniques, encrusted enamel on gold; the finest surviving examples were made around 1400. The gold sceptre which Charles V had made for his son's coronation is one of the earliest examples of the technique: the fleur-de-lis in the middle part was originally covered with a layer of opaque white enamel.

Quatrefoil diptych
Paris, c. 1370-1380
Detail
Ivory. Height 20.3 cm; width (open) 22.5 cm
Acquired in 1900
OA 4089

Pair of valves of a mirror: Christ between
St John the Baptist and St Charlemagne;
the Virgin between St Catherine and St John
Paris, before 1379
Gold, translucent basse-taille enamel
Diameter 6.8 cm
Provenance, treasury of Louis I of Anjou, brother of King Charles V
Formerly Durand collection
Acquired in 1825
MR 2608-2609

Charles V's sceptre
Paris, 1365–1380
Gold, formerly enamelled (fleur-de-lis), pearls,
precious stones
Overall height 60 cm
Entrusted in 1380 to the treasury of Saint-Denis
by Charles V for use at the coronation of his son,
the future Charles VI
MS 83

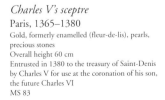

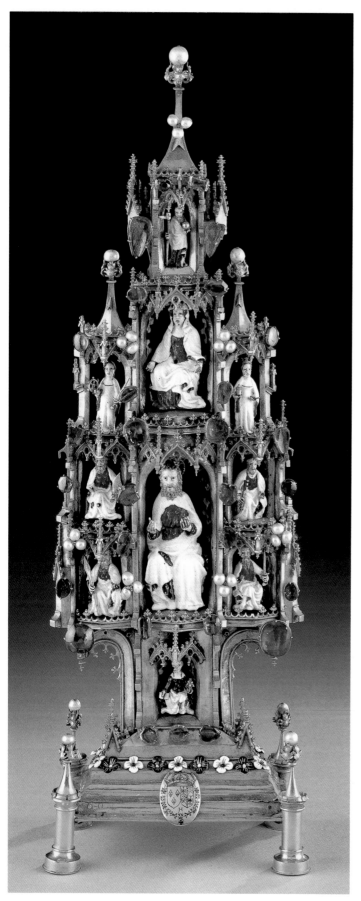

Ewer bearing the Bourbon arms
Paris, 14th century (crystal);
15th century
(mount)
Rock crystal, silver-gilt,
precious stones
Height 29 cm
Formerly collection of Louis XIV
OA 29

Reliquary picture from treasury of
the Order of the Saint-Esprit
London (?), before 1412
Silver-gilt, enamels on gold, pearls and precious stones
Height 44.5 cm
Provenance, treasury of the Order of the Saint-Esprit
MR 552

Offering of the heart
Arras (?), c. 1400–1410
Tapestry, wool. Height 247 cm; width 210 cm
C. Davillier bequest, 1883
OA 3131

Bowl with coat of arms of Florence
Tuscany,
second quarter of 15th century
Faience. Diameter 64 cm
Acquired in 1897
OA 3946

Plate "Hispano-Moresque"
Valence, c. 1420–1430
Lustre faience. Diameter 48 cm
J.-L. Leroux bequest, 1897
OA 4028

Prophet
By Guillaume Boey,
Gautier Dufour and Jean de Clichy
Paris, 1409
Gilt-bronze. Height 14 cm
From the base of the reliquary of
St Germanus at Saint-Germain-des-Prés
J. Maciet gift, 1903
OA 5917

Self-portrait of Jean Fouquet
By Jean Fouquet (c. 1415/1420–c. 1480)
c. 1450
Copper, gold-painted enamel. Diameter 6.8 cm
From the frame of the diptych of Notre-Dame of Melun
commissioned by Etienne Chevalier, secretary and counsellor
to King Charles VII
H. de Janzé gift, 1861
OA 56

Jean Fouquet, the greatest French painter of the fifteenth century, embodies a special trend in French art which rejects the excesses of Flamboyant art, and reveals some Italian influence. The Melun diptych – one half is now in Berlin, the other in Antwerp – had a series of medallions on its frame, including the self-portrait in the Louvre, the first self-portrait in Western painting and the painter's autograph signature, an «incunabulum» of the enamelling technique which was to prosper in Limoges from the late fifteenth century. The painter applied a first layer of black enamel to a copper plate, then a grey-brown scumble and finally a layer of gold which he scratched with a needle to produce the effect of a gold cameo on a black ground.

Coronation of the Virgin
By the Master of the Louis XII Triptych
Limoges, c. 1500
Enamels painted on copper. Diameter 23 cm
Old collection
N. 1218

*Reliquary angels of
Anne de Bretagne*
France,
mid-14th and
mid-15th century
Silver-gilt, rock crystal.
Height 43.5 cm and 43.8 cm
Provenance, treasury of
the Order of the Saint-Esprit
MR 550 and 551

Working with wool
France, first quarter of 16th century
Millefleurs tapestry
Wool. Height 220 cm; width 319 cm
Larcade gift, 1945
OA 9408

The rise of tapestry as an art form is one of the most remarkable artistic phenomenons of the late Gothic period. While Paris seems to have played a role in prompting this upsurge – the famous set of tapestries relating to *The Apocalypse* now in Angers was made there between 1373 and 1380 – Flanders and the Low Countries were pre-eminent from the mid-fifteenth century. What are described as mille-fleurs tapestries where elegant figures are depicted against a ground strewn with flowers are among its most attractive products. *Working with wool*, featuring the arms of Thomas Bohier – the former chamberlain of King Charles VIII who started building the Château de Chenonceau in 1515 – and Catherine Briçonnet, is one of a set of hangings inspired by the literary theme of the pastoral where the games and activities of the peasants and gentry are interspersed.

The Italian Renaissance

From the beginning of the fifteenth century architects, sculptors and painters in Tuscany were at the forefront of an enthusiastic and deliberate return to Antiquity which led to a decisive break with the traditions of International Gothic art. The famous competition for the doors of the baptistery of the cathedral in Florence in 1402 which was won by Ghiberti, the construction of the cathedral dome by Brunelleschi started in 1418 and Masaccio's frescoes at Santa Maria del Carmine in 1426–1427 meant that this early Renaissance first emerged in Florence, rapidly spreading throughout Italy in the course of the century.

Sculptors played a crucial role in the genesis of this new art, as can easily be seen from the collection of Italian Renaissance bronzes held by the Department of Objets d'Art, one of the finest in the world. Donatello (d. 1466), a pupil of Ghiberti to whom a remarkable *Crucifixion* can be ascribed, goes beyond Gothic realism, treating his figures in a monumental manner and systematically exploring space by means of perspective. Bellano (d. 1496/97), a native of Padua trained by Donatello, who worked mainly in Padua, extended his master's experiments in a narrative spirit very much his own, with touches that are sometimes intimist, as illustrated by his *St Jerome and the lion*. And finally Andrea Briosco known as Riccio (d. 1532), a pupil of Bellano and a Paduan like him, achieved formal perfection c. 1500 with his *Arion*, an emblematic representation of the Greek poet who, according to Aristotle, was saved from drowning by a dolphin delighting in his poetry: antique, mythological inspiration here becomes elegiac and intellectual. The great lessons learnt and assimilated from Antiquity are also manifest in the group of eight large bas-reliefs from the tomb of Girolamo and Marcantonio della Torre, a major work undertaken by Riccio after 1511 for the church of San Fermo Maggiore in Verona; the humanist ideal of the Renaissance is confidently expressed, right down to the presence of *putti* playing at the foot of the grave in the funeral scene.

A similar triumphant abundance can be found on the famous wedding cup in blue Venetian glass with an enamelled decoration depicting an allegorical procession in limpid colours, which is reminiscent of the graceful compositions of Botticelli. It is also expressed on the majolica made in the various great Italian centres; the Louvre possesses a fine collection of majolica. Starting at the end of the fifteenth century in Faenza – from which the word "faience" is derived – a new type of ceramics appeared, *istoriato*, where a painted decoration depicts scenes that tell a story. This genre was quickly copied, reaching its peak in Urbino in the Marches in the early sixteenth century with Nicola da Urbino, who was responsible for the plate from the service of Isabella D'Este, made c. 1525, depicting *Abilemech spying on Isaac and Rebekah* after a composition by Raphael at the Vatican, and Francesco Xanto Avelli who created the two plaques illustrating the *Childhood of Cyrus*, signed and dated 1536, in which secular iconography and rustic inspiration

Arion
By Andrea Briosco known as Riccio (1470–1532)
Padua, c. 1500
Bronze. Height 25 cm
C. Davillier gift
OA 9115

51

are intermingled. At Castel Durante near Urbino artists abandoned their original preference for an ornamental style to make a speciality of bust portraits of women (*belle donne*) and heroes from Antiquity – these occupy every inch of available space, as on the cup celebrating *Cornelius*, c. 1525–1530; for their part, the artists of Deruta in Umbria who often treated the same subjects gave added brilliancy to their creations through a metallic lustre with yellow highlights, sometimes tinging their work with humour as on the large plate depicting an unfaithful wife suspended by her feet, dated 1510. However in the mid-sixteenth century changing taste led to *istorati* being gradually dropped in favour of purely ornamental compositions with Mannerist decorations of grotesques on a white ground, based on those executed by Raphael. The workshop of the Patanazzi of Urbino is one of the finest representatives of this type of work, with pieces from the service of Alfonso II D'Este, Duke of Ferrara, made c. 1579.

But from the very beginning of the sixteenth century the genius of Michelangelo (d. 1564) had contributed to the development of a Mannerist trend which was to influence Italian sculpture profoundly. The famous *Gnome with the snail* made in northern Italy c. 1530–1550 and the telamon created by the Paduan Zoppo c. 1560–1565, a replica of a vanquished Turk made of marble intended for the tomb of Alessandro Contarini at the Santo in Padua, are indicative of a restless artistic sensibility and a search for pathetic expression. At the end of the century the Frenchman Giambologna, who settled in Florence in 1561 in the service of the Medicis and worked in Italy throughout his career, produced one of the masterpieces of this trend, a bronze depicting Deianeira being snatched by the Centaur Nessus, which is signed on the centaur's head-band and was made c. 1580.

Princely caprice also explains how such strange works as the "Medici porcelain" came to be made, sumptuous pieces imitating Chinese porcelain with a blue decoration on a white ground; only a few examples were made in Florence, probably from 1575 on, for Grand Duke Francesco I de' Medici. Ercole II D'Este was no doubt motivated by similar reasons when he subverted a German weaver Hans Karcher, setting him up in Ferrara; in 1545 Karcher made a set of tapestries based on Ovid's *Metamorphoses*, after cartoons by the painter Battista Dossi – a pretext for depicting the gardens of aristocrats. It was again princes who jealously collected large *pietre dure* vases in mounts of precious metals, like their predecessors in the Middle Ages. They promoted the growth of lapidaries' workshops in Milan in particular, where outstanding pieces were cut from jasper or rock crystal, such as the crystal cup depicting the *Story of Noah* which came into the possession of Louis XIV a century later.

Bas-relief: Crucifixion
Ascribed to Donatello (1386–1466)
Italy, c. 1440
Bronze. Height 42 cm; width 29 cm
I. de Camondo bequest, 1911
OA 6477

St Jerome and the lion
Ascribed to Bartolomeo Bellano
(c. 1440–1496/97)
Padua, c. 1490–1495
Bronze. Height 25 cm
Mme G. Dreyfus gift, 1919
OA 7250

Bas-relief from the tomb of della Torres:
Funeral
By Andrea Briosco, known as Riccio (1470–1532)
Padua, 1516–1521
Bronze. Height 37 cm; width 49 cm
Provenance, tomb of Girolamo and Marcantonio della Torre at
San Fermo Maggiore, Verona
OA 9096

Both bronze and marble were admirably well suited to re-
viving the art of bas-relief. The eight bas-reliefs on the tomb
of the Della Torres in Verona, one of Riccio's main works,
are a virtual manifesto of the Renaissance, with the
humanist preoccupations derived from Antiquity taking
over from traditional religious convictions. Girolamo and
Marcantonio Della Torre taught medicine at the University
of Padua, as we are reminded by the first four bas-reliefs
which recount the life and death of a professor of medicine;
the other four describe the journey of the soul to under-
world, after Virgil. (After the funeral scene the soul, represented by a winged *putto* holding a book, is first welcomed
by Charon on the banks of the Styx, then in the mythological Elysian Fields, before finally returning to earth to enjoy
posthumous fame.)

*Cup decorated with
an allegorical procession*
Venice, c. 1500
Enamelled glass. Height 17.5 cm
Baronne S. de Rothschild bequest, 1922
OA 7564

*Plate with an allegorical
decoration*
Deruta, 1510
Lustre faience. Diameter 56 cm
Acquired in 1938
OA 9205

Cup: Cornelius
Ascribed to the workshop
of Giovanni Maria Vasaro
Castel Durante, c. 1525-1530
Faience. Diameter 20.5 cm
Former Campana collection
Acquired in 1861
OA 1745

Gnome with the snail
Northern Italy,
first half of 16th century
Bronze with black patina.
Height 37.5 cm
Acquired in 1933
OA 8252

Plaques: Childhood of Cyrus
By Francesco Xanto Avelli
Urbino, 1536
Faience. Height 30 cm; width 27.8 cm
Acquired in 1937
OA 9028 and 9029

Plate from service of Isabella D'Este:
Abimelech spying on Isaac and Rebekah
By Nicola da Urbino (fl. between 1520 and 1545),
after Raphael
Urbino, c. 1525
Faience. Diameter 33 cm
Baronne S. de Rothschild bequest, 1922
OA 7578

Fall of Phaeton
One of a set of tapestries illustrating Ovid's
Metamorphoses, after Battista Dossi
(after 1490–1542) made for Ercolo II D'Este-Ferrara
Workshop of Hans Karcher, 1545
Tapestry, wool and silk. Height 480 cm; width 500 cm
Deposited by the Mobilier National, 1946
Gob. 124

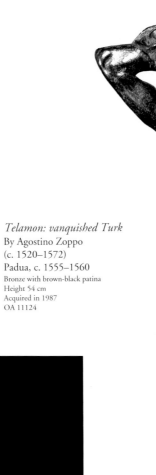

Telamon: vanquished Turk
By Agostino Zoppo
(c. 1520–1572)
Padua, c. 1555–1560
Bronze with brown-black patina
Height 54 cm
Acquired in 1987
OA 11124

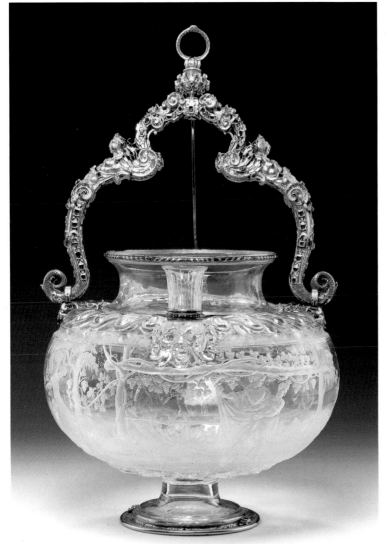

Cup: Story of Noah
Italy, mid-16th century
Rock crystal, enamelled gold handle
Height 42 cm; width 25 cm
Formerly collection of Louis XIV
MR 285

Nessus and Deianeira
By Giambologna (1529–1608)
Florence, c. 1580
Bronze with brown-red patina, signed
Height 42.1 cm
Given to Louis XIV by Le Nôtre; formerly Crown collection
OA 9480

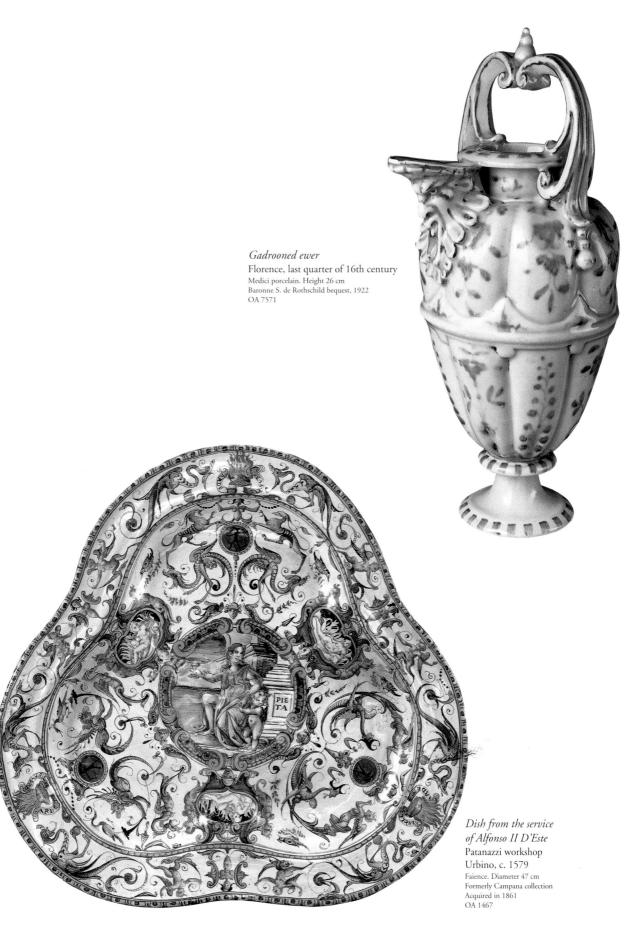

Gadrooned ewer
Florence, last quarter of 16th century
Medici porcelain. Height 26 cm
Baronne S. de Rothschild bequest, 1922
OA 7571

*Dish from the service
of Alfonso II D'Este*
Patanazzi workshop
Urbino, c. 1579
Faience. Diameter 47 cm
Formerly Campana collection
Acquired in 1861
OA 1467

The Renaissance
in France and Europe

The Italian wars waged in the reigns of Charles VIII (1483–1498) and Louis XII (1498–1515) played a crucial role in introducing the first Renaissance forms into France. As in architecture and monumental decoration, artists were initially content to superimpose Italian-inspired elements on works that were still medieval in spirit. Thus the Master of the Louis XII Triptych, one of the most gifted Limoges enamellers of his generation, had no scruples about giving his *Mater dolorosa* at prayer, a medieval subject expressed in a style close to that of the painter Jean Bourdichon, a border of cherubs and garlands, motifs obviously taken from Italian books in Louis XII's library at Blois.

But it was mainly from the time of François I (1515–1547) and in the reign of Henri II (1547–1559) that the first French Renaissance flourished. The "Fontainebleau" School, associated with the building work at the royal Château of Fontainebleau where French artists worked alongside Italians such as Rosso, Primaticcio or Niccolo dell'Abbate, created an Italianizing French style characterized by fresh colours, an elegant, sometimes Mannerist gracefulness in the figures, a generalized liking for architecture shown in perspective, and wide borders of fruit and strapwork. The tapestry depicting St Mamas giving himself up to the court presided over by the governor of Cappadocia, which comes from a set of wall hangings ordered by Cardinal Claude de Longwy for Langres cathedral after cartoons by Jean Cousin the elder (d. 1560) and woven in Paris in 1544, illustrates the school's wide sphere of influence, as – on a more modest scale – does the delicate decoration engraved on the spherical watch made by Jacques de La Garde. Made at Blois in 1551, it is the oldest signed and dated French watch.

Engraving experienced its golden age in France at this period, contributing greatly to making the art of the Fontainebleau School more widely known. Etienne Delaune (d. 1583), who engraved the works of Primaticcio and dell'Abbate, was responsible for designs for Henri II's armour, decorated in the Fontainebleau spirit with scenes from the story of Caesar and Pompey. Delaune's style can also be recognized on gold and silverware and jewellery, for example the enamelled gold setting of a pendant with two figures of Peace on either side of a cameo carved with a nymph astride a hippocampus. The influence of the Fontainebleau School dominated the century: the masks, strapwork and fruit on Charles IX's shield – made of iron covered with partly enamelled gold, illustrating Marius's victory over Jugurtha, king of Numidia – which the widow of the Parisian goldsmith Pierre Redon delivered in 1572 still conform to its aesthetic canon. In a parallel development the work of architects like Androuet du Cerceau or Hugues Sambin which was widely distributed in engravings had an impact even on furniture: thus the Arconati Visconti armoire, partly painted and gilded, is decorated with three terms with satyrs' and female fauns' heads close to models published by Sambin.

Anne de Montmorency, Constable of France
By Léonard Limosin
(c. 1505–1576)
Limoges, 1556
Enamel on copper, gilded wood
Height 72 cm
Acquired in 1794
N 1254

63

The Limoges workshops producing enamel painted on copper were at the height of their powers in the mid-sixteenth century. Various shaped pieces, plates, ewers, bowls, caskets and plaques depict biblical, antique or mythological scenes in colour or grisaille: the Louvre's collection is one of the finest in the world. The two roundels decorated with battle scenes in grisaille after Giulio Romano show the enamellers' consummate skill and their perfect assimilation of the lessons of the Renaissance. The greatest enameller of all, Léonard Limosin (d. c. 1576), worked for the court and created enamel portraits. His masterpiece is the portrait of Anne de Montmorency, Constable of France; it is signed and dated 1556 and has kept its original frame on which the satyrs in grisaille are inspired by those in the François Premier Gallery at Fontainebleau.

The Louvre also has an excellent collection of French Renaissance ceramics. The impetus derived from Italian models is obvious in the first works produced by French ceramicists, as in the decoration of the altar step from the Château de La Bâtie d'Urfé made by Masséot Abaquesne in Rouen – he opened a faience factory there c. 1530. But French artists soon established their independence. From the 1550s they used a white clay decorated with brown patterns and the forms employed in goldsmithing in the extremely rare pieces known as "Saint-Porchaire" pottery; with Bernard Palissy they invented extraordinary relief patterns on glazed earthenware pots, tortured in appearance, full of plants, reptiles or crustaceans which seem to be modelled from nature, or made moulds to create relief models of subjects inspired from engravings, such as the allegory of Water, a favourite theme of the Fontainebleau School, framed by lines written by Du Bartas.

A remarkable group of silverware was created thanks to the foundation of the Order of the Saint-Esprit in 1578 in the troubled reign of Henri III (1574–1589). The Order's treasure which is now in the Louvre was partly made up of earlier pieces taken from the royal treasure, such as the crystal and silver gilt ciborium crowned by a figure of St Helen which was made in Paris in the 1530s, as well as works specifically created for it such as the mace made in Paris in 1584–1585. Four bas-reliefs based on drawings by Toussaint Dubreuil in a frame with overtones of classical architecture highlight various episodes in the Order's ceremonial proceedings, with all the ease that typifies the Fontainebleau style.

The Louvre's collections also enable us to appreciate the impact of Italian art elsewhere in Europe, in the Netherlands and Germany in particular. The magnificent set of hangings illustrating *The hunts of Maximilian* woven in Brussels between 1531 and 1533 after cartoons by Bernard Van Orley (d. 1541), a painter who worked in the service of the Habsburgs, combines Italian humanist inspiration and Flemish descriptive traditions with consummate skill. The vessels known as the ewer and dish of Emperor Charles V, made in Antwerp in 1558–1559, immortalizing the emperor's siege of Tunis in 1535, make rich use of the art of bas-relief and of themes common throughout Renaissance Europe, such as the bust of a woman with a shell as a head-dress. By the end of the century an intimate knowledge of Italian art was general at European courts, as symbolized by the monumental bloodstone cup carved by Ottavio Miseroni in 1608 in Prague, the residence of Emperor Rudolf II.

Mater dolorosa at prayer
Ascribed to the Master of the Louis XII Triptych
Limoges, beginning of 16th century
Polychrome enamels on copper
Height 30 cm
Acquired in 1988
OA 11170

Ciborium from the treasury of the Order of the Saint-Esprit
Paris, c. 1530
Rock crystal, silver-gilt, enamel, precious stones, pearls, cameos
Height 33 cm
Provenance, treasury of the Order of the Saint-Esprit
MR 547

Spherical watch
By Jacques de La Garde
Blois, 1551
Gilt copper. Diameter 5.3 cm
P. Garnier gift, 1916
OA 7019

St Mamas giving himself up to the court
of the governor of Cappadocia
One of a set of hangings illustrating the story of St Mamas
made for Langres cathedral after Jean Cousin the elder
(c. 1490–c. 1560)
Paris, 1544
Tapestry, wool. Height 440 cm; width 450 cm
M.-L.-M. Lereuil gift, 1940
OA 9327

SAINCT MAMES APRES AVOYR FESTIEE ET SE ESTRE DECLARE A CEVLX
QVI LE VOVLOYENT PRANDRE AYANS DIFFERE POVR LA PEVR QVILZ
HEVRENT DES BESTES : DE LVY MESMES AVEC VNG LYON SEN ALLA
PRESENTER AV DVC ALEXANDRE QVI LE FEIST MARTIRISER ·

*Pendant: Nymph astride
a hippocampus*
Paris, c. 1560
Cameo, enamelled gold.
Height 11.2 cm
Mme B. de Rothschild gift, 1974
OA 10587

Ewer with the letter G
Workshop known as Saint-Porchaire,
c. 1550
"Saint-Porchaire" ceramics. Height 37.2 cm
Mme J. Piatigorski gift, 1975
OA 10589

Roundel: battle scene
Ascribed to Pierre Pénicaud (1515–after 1590)
Limoges, mid-16th century
Grisaille enamel painted on copper
Diameter 40 cm
Formerly Durand collection
Acquired in 1825
MR 2521

The set of hangings of *The hunts of Maximilian* became part of the royal collections in the reign of Louis XIV. They are exceptional for the fineness of the weaving which uses gold and silver thread, and take their name from one of the most celebrated huntsmen of the period, Emperor Maximilian, the grandfather of Emperor Charles V. The set consists of twelve tapestries illustrating hunting scenes in the forests round Brussels appropriate to each month of the year. They start with March which was then the first month in the civil year, symbolized at the top centre of the border by the sign of the ram, while the landscape is a very accurate view of the town of Brussels, from the former ducal palace on the left to the towers of Sainte-Gudule on the right.

The month of March
First in a set of tapestries known as *The hunts of Maximilian*, after Bernard Van Orley (c. 1488–1541)
Brussels, c. 1528–1533
Tapestry, wool, silk, gold and silver thread
Height 440 cm; width 750 cm
Formerly royal collections
OA 7314

*Vessels known as the ewer and dish of
Charles V: Capture of Tunis in 1535*
Antwerp, 1558–1559
Silver-gilt, (ewer) partly enamelled
Height of ewer 43.5 cm; diameter of dish 64 cm
Formerly collection of the Princes of Chimay
Came to the Louvre in 1795
MR 341 and 351

Altar step from La Bâtie d'Urfé
Detail
By Masséot Abaquesne (d. before 1564)
Rouen, 1557
Overall height 185 cm; overall length 320 cm; side of a tile 11 cm
Gift of Beurdeley senior and junior, 1880
OA 2518

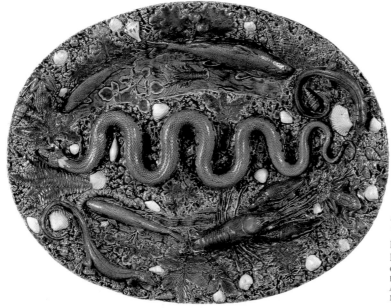

Large oval dish with a decoration of
"rustic figulines"
By Bernard Palissy (c. 1510-1590)
France, c. 1560
Glazed terracotta. Length 52.5 cm
Formerly Durand collection
Acquired in 1825
MR 2293

*Ceremonial mace of the Order
of the Saint-Esprit*
Bas-relief after drawings
by Toussaint Dubreuil (c. 1561–1602)
Paris, 1584–1585
Enamelled silver-gilt. Height 110 cm
Provenance, treasury of the Order of the Saint-Esprit
MR 564

*Charles IX's shield:
Marius's victory over Jugurtha, King of Numidia*
By Pierre Redon (d. 1572)
Paris, c. 1572
Repoussé gold-plated iron, enamel
Height 68 cm; width 49 cm
Formerly Crown collection
MR 426

*Armoire known as
Hugues Sambin's*
France, c. 1580
Partly gilded and painted oak
and walnut
Height 206 cm; width 150 cm
Gift of Marchesa Arconati Visconti,
1916
OA 6968

Plaque: allegory of water
France, c. 1580–1590
Glazed earthenware. Height 42.6 cm;
width 52 cm
Acquired in 1893
OA 3363

*Emperor
Rudolf II's cup*
By Ottavio Miseroni
(d. 1624)
Prague, 1608
Bloodstone, silver-gilt.
Length 57.5 cm
Formerly Crown collection
MR 143

The century of Louis XIV

Although the reign of Henri IV (1589–1610) is still in many ways marked by Renaissance art, it brings that period to an end – the final impact of the Renaissance barely extending beyond the start of the seventeenth century. The statues of the king and Queen Marie de Medici as Jupiter and Juno by Barthélémy Prieur (d. 1611) still adhere to a Mannerist canon, but the serene gravity of the figures already anticipates the Classical age, while the idealized image of the royal couple is indicative of the beginning of a tendency to exalt the monarchy which was taken to the ultimate extreme by Louis XIV. The profuse carving on the Révoil armoire dated 1617 is still inspired by engravings, in this case those of Spranger and De Vos; by the very exuberance of its decoration it is already veering towards the Baroque.

The dual trends of Baroque and Classical which ushered in the seventeenth century in France were not yet in competition with one another, and in the reign of Louis XIII (1610–1643) and until the middle of the century they carried on side by side, or mingled with one another. When Simon Vouet, the most influential painter of his day, was recalled from Rome by the king in 1627, he went beyond his Caravaggesque experience, moving on to a fluid, elegant and luminous style which is gracefully expressed on the tapestry of *Moses rescued from the waters of the Nile*, part of a set of hangings illustrating the Story of the Old Testament, made from models which the king – whose monogram and motto appear on the tapestries – had commissioned from Vouet. The tapestry was woven at the Louvre c. 1630, and is evidence of a constant political concern, starting with Sully, that France should have distinguished factories of its own, an undertaking that Louis XIV and Colbert finally achieved with the success of the royal factories. Two pieces made in the workshops of Parisian goldsmiths in the 1630s, on the other hand, are typified by Baroque richness and caprice: the piece known as the candlestick of Marie de Medici which is completely covered with cameos and brightly coloured *pietre dure*, and even more so the extraordinary ewer by Pierre Delabarre – the goldsmith has taken a damaged antique carved sard vase and cleverly hidden the defects with a mount made of enamelled gold highlighted with precious stones, providing a handle in the form of a polychrome dragon and a lid which is itself made of skilfully arranged fragments of sard, crowned by a white-enamelled helmeted head of Minerva. Other goldsmiths like the unidentified maker of the gold box known as Anne of Austria's casket preferred to seek their inspiration in nature; large scrolls of flowers and foliage made in embossed and chased openwork gold produce an ornamental embroidered effect which was particularly popular in the middle of the century. The taste for embroidered motifs is also reflected in the famous furniture from the château of Marshal d'Effiat dating from the 1660s, armchairs and a bed with a tester which still have their original upholstery of cut Genoa velvet. From the beginning of the seventeenth century, however, *ébénisterie*, a technique that involves concealing the pine

Armoire
By André-Charles Boulle (1642–1732)
Paris, c. 1700
Ebony and amaranth veneer, marquetry of polychrome woods, brass, pewter, tortoiseshell and horn on a wooden carcase, gilt-bronze
Height 255.5 cm; width 157.5 cm
Transferred from the Mobilier National, 1870
OA 5516

or oak carcase of a piece of furniture under a luxurious veneer of precious woods, began to appear in France, as evidenced by the ebony cabinet in the Louvre, a Parisian piece made in the mid-seventeenth century which combines religious and mythological bas-reliefs with the naturalist plant decoration fashionable at the time.

The long reign of Louis XIV (1643–1715) whose period of personal rule started in 1661 was the point at which France was supreme in Europe, and corresponds with the definition of French Classicism which generally abjured the Baroque excesses prevalent elsewhere. This was partly due to the activity of the Academies, partly to the way the royal factories were organized – the king gave them his protection and granted them privileges and in return they glorified him – and finally partly to the unifying role played by the painter Charles Le Brun (d. 1690). He was the founder of the Académie de Peinture et de Sculpture, and was put in charge of the Gobelins factory and given overall responsibility for all royal works involving art; this resulted in an undeniable unity of style. The Savonnerie factory which was established in Paris in 1667 produced magnificent carpets such as those intended for the Grande Galerie in the Louvre made c. 1670–1680, on which large symmetrical scrolls frame the arms and subjects of the symbolism of royalty. The Gobelins factory set up by Colbert in 1667 brought together all the arts and crafts, but remains famous for its manufacture of tapestries: original creations such as the set of tapestries relating the *King's Story*, or copies of older hangings such as the *Story of Scipio* after Giulio Romano, woven in 1688–1690. The Italian glassmaker Bernardo Perroto who was established by letters patent in Orleans from 1662 introduced the process of making pressed glass into France, which the "Manufacture des Glaces" set up in 1665 and transferred to Saint-Gobain in 1685 took over from him in 1695. Ceramic workshops in Nevers that had existed for a long time under the king's protection made use of the forms created by goldsmiths, as in the large pair of ewers made c. 1675 based on a bronze model made by Claude Ballin the elder for the gardens at Versailles.

The military disasters and difficulties marking the end of Louis XIV's reign led to the disappearance of almost all the silverware belonging to the king; it was melted down. Very few works escaped the crucible; among them is the Grand Dauphin's silver-gilt bowl made by Sébastien Leblond in 1690–1692 where a rich chased and engraved decoration of plants and animals is strictly ordered. A few small objects in gold or silver such as the gold watch made by François-Joseph de Camus in 1709 for Louis-Léon Pajot, a member of the French Academy, nonetheless give us some idea of what the works that have disappeared must have looked like. The king's silver furniture met the same fate. So it became necessary to invent furniture that was fit for the king, but made of less valuable materials. André-Charles Boulle (1642–1732) had perfected a new kind of marquetry made of copper, brass, tortoiseshell and coloured wood, highlighted with gilt-bronze mounts. Thus the large armoire at the Louvre, probably made in the final years of the king's reign, combining Boulle marquetry and floral marquetry of exceptional delicacy lies at the very start of the extraordinary development of French furniture in the eighteenth century.

Armoire in two sections
France, first quarter of 17th century
Walnut. Height 254 cm; width 185 cm
Formerly Révoil collection
Acquired in 1828
MRR 61

Henri IV as Jupiter
and Marie de Medici as Juno
By Barthélemy Prieur (1536–1611)
Paris, 1600–1610
Bronze with brown patina, signed
Height 63.5 and 67 cm
Acquired in 1986
OA 11054 and 11055

Ewer
By Pierre Delabarre (fl. 1625–1654)
Stone: 1st century BC or AD
Mount: Paris, c. 1630
Sard, enamelled gold. Height 28 cm
Formerly collection of Louis XIV
MR 445

Marie de Medici's candlestick
Paris, c. 1630
Silver-gilt, cameos, sards. Height 45 cm
Formerly Crown collection
MR 251

Moses rescued from the waters
One of a set of tapestries illustrating *The story of the Old Testament* made after the modelli commissioned by Louis XIII from the painter Simon Vouet in 1627
Paris, c. 1630
Wool and silk tapestry
Height 495 cm; width 588 cm
Transferred from the Mobilier National, 1901
Inv. 6086

This tapestry immortalizing the discovery of Moses by Pharaoh's daughter by the banks of the Nile was actually woven at the Louvre; it illustrates the king's desire to promote French art independent of great foreign centres and is indicative of the revival of Parisian art at the king's instigation in the first half of the seventeenth century. The arms of France and Navarre at the top centre of the border of grotesques, punctuated at the corners by antique-style profiles, the king's cypher – an L topped by the closed crown – at the sides, and the club of Hercules and the personal motto of the king at the bottom centre are insistent reminders of the sovereign's role.

Gold casket known as
Anne of Austria's casket
Paris, mid-17th century
Repoussé and chased gold on wooden core
Height 22 cm; width 45 cm
Formerly Crown collection
MR 159

Tester bed from the Château d'Effiat
France, c. 1650
Natural walnut, cut Genoa silk velvet
and embroidered silk fabrics
Height 295 cm
Formerly Du Sommerard collection,
on deposit at the Louvre
C1 2550

Cabinet
Paris, c. 1645
Ebony veneer on an oak and poplar carcase;
blackened fruitwood base
Height 184 cm; width 158.5 cm
Formerly Révoil collection
Acquired in 1828
MRR 62

Medallion: Louis XIV
By Bernard Perrot
(Bernardo Perroto) (1638–1709)
Orleans, c. 1680
Pressed glass. Height 37 cm
Honda-France gift, 1993
OA 11378

Pair of ewers
Nevers, c. 1675
Faience. Height 60.5 cm
A. Gérard bequest, 1900
OA 5013

*Carpet for the Grande Galerie
du Louvre with the coat
of arms of Louis XIV*
Paris, Savonnerie factory,
c. 1670–1680
Wool. Length 895 cm; width 510 cm
Transferred from the Mobilier National, 1901
OA 5432 bis A

"Onion" watch
By François-Joseph de Camus
(1672–1732)
Paris, 1709
Gold, gilt brass, enamel. Diameter 6.2 cm
Olivier bequest, 1935
OA 8310

*Bowl belonging to the Grand
Dauphin, Louis XIV's son*
By Sébastien Leblond (fl. 1674–1715)
Paris, 1690–1692
Silver-gilt. Width 29.8 cm; diameter of lid 18 cm
Corroyer gift, 1923
OA 7757

The battle of Zama
Tenth in a set of tapestries
illustrating *The Story of Scipio*
After Giulio Romano (1499–1549)
Paris, c. 1688–1690
Wool tapestry. Height 435 cm; width 740 cm
Transferred from the Mobilier National, 1901
OA 5394

Louvois had the idea of having copies made of some of the finest Renaissance tapestries as a way of overcoming financial problems at the Gobelins factory c. 1680–1690, so ensuring that the weavers had work without having to pay artists for new models. This is how a set of hangings from Louis XIV's collections bearing the arms of Jacques d'Albon, Maréchal de Saint-André, came to be copied; they themselves were made after the set of gold and silk hangings of *Scipio Africanus Major* which had belonged to François I and were destroyed at the time of the Revolution. Each tapestry illustrates an episode from the story of the Second Punic War between Rome and Carthage and the victory of Scipio Africanus as told by Livy. (The tenth tapestry, the Battle of Zama where Scipio finally defeated Hannibal, shows the front line of the Carthaginian army with its threatening elephants which were soon to turn against the Carthaginians themselves in response to the racket made by the Romans.)

The eighteenth century

Like classical Greek sculpture or Italian Renaissance painting, the French decorative arts of the eighteenth century are universally renowned. There is not a museum in the world where they are not represented. The conjuncture of a prosperous economy, a long tradition in the arts and crafts, an imaginative trade policy for art, enlightened patrons and great creative artists – painters like Boucher, sculptors like Falconet, ornamenters, *ébénistes*, bronziers (makers of bronze furnishings), goldsmiths – successfully led to an increase in the output of works in every field. There were four successive trends which overlapped one another, usually known as the "Régence" (French Regency), rocaille or Louis XV, Greek or transition, and Louis XVI styles.

Although Louis XIV had disappeared from the scene, the Crown still pursued a policy emphasizing its own prestige, as evidenced by the purchase of the "Régent" diamond in 1717. It was first used on the silver-gilt crown of the young Louis XV, who was crowned in 1722. Although furniture at this time was still imbued with the grandeur typical of Louis XIV, as the armchairs made c. 1710–1720 for the financier Pierre Crozat demonstrate, lines were becoming more curved. Where *ébénisterie* was concerned, Boulle marquetry was still its most luxurious manifestation, but was soon to be supplanted by the beautiful geometric veneers with a more muted polychromy which decorate Cressent's works or the bureau bearing the stamp of Dubois. The king himself gave the art of furniture-making a huge boost when he started taking a personal interest in the furnishing of his residences in the late 1730s, as illustrated by the lacquer commode by B.V.R.B. delivered to him in 1737. The Marquise de Pompadour's liaison with the king dates from 1745 and from then on she contributed towards strengthening this interest. Although the *Four Seasons* from Rouen with their high-fired decoration or the Camondo hanging wall-clock which is typical of the low-fired polychrome decoration first appearing in Strasbourg in the middle of the century brilliantly demonstrate the continuing importance of faience, the eighteenth century is the century of porcelain. The king and Madame de Pompadour's predilection for the Vincennes porcelain factory which was founded in 1745, transferred to Sèvres in 1756 and turned into a "manufacture royale" in 1759, is symbolized by the pot-pourri vase which belonged to the King's favourite. The king could also call on the royal factories already in existence, the Gobelins and the Savonnerie.

The collections at the Louvre provide sufficient evidence that the royal princes as well as the king were great lovers and collectors of art. It must surely have been the Comte de Toulouse, a son of Louis XIV, who commissioned Thomas Germain to make the bottle seals in the service that later belonged to his son, the Duc de Penthièvre. The epergne by Röettiers bears the arms of the Duc de Bourbon, while the tapestries recounting the *Story of Don Quixote* were ordered from the Gobelins by the Duc d'Orléans, the

Madame Du Barry's commode
Attributed to Martin Carlin (1730–1785)
Paris, 1772
Detail
Pearwood, tulipwood and amaranth veneer on an oak carcase, soft-paste Sèvres porcelain plaques (after Jean-Baptiste Pater, Nicolas Lancret and Carle van Loo), gilt-bronze, white marble
Height 87 cm; width 119 cm
Dation in payment of capital transfer taxes, 1990
OA 11293

Regent's son. The pair of andirons designed and proudly signed by François-Thomas Germain were made in 1757 for his son, the next Duc d'Orléans.

The great Parisian *marchands merciers* (licensed dealers) managed to impose coordination on the compartmented guilds. We are reminded of the role of the *marchands merciers* by a few important works: Thomas-Joachim Hébert, one of the first people to make furniture veneered with oriental lacquers, supplied the commode by B.V.R.B. already mentioned, with its slender rocaille bronze furnishings; Lazare Duvaux bought the *Naiad* from Sèvres in 1757 then sold it to Hébert who must have been responsible for its beautiful bronze mount, typical of a more mature rocaille style; Simon-Philippe Poirier commissioned the first pieces of furniture decorated with plaques of Sèvres porcelain, including the vernis Martin chiffonnière by B.V.R.B.

This Parisian art gradually spread to the provinces. The Marquis de Sourches had the wood panelling and the various chairs for the large drawing-room at Château d'Abondant (Eure-et-Loir) made in Paris between 1747 and 1750, while the armchairs by Heurtaut which probably belonged to Monseigneur de Sainte-Aulaire, Bishop of Poitiers, came from Paris.

The furniture designed by the architect Le Lorrain for Lalive de Jully made c. 1757 was the manifesto of a rebellion by some creative artists against the rocaille style. For a period of about fifteen years there was then a vogue for rectilinear, architectural furniture in the "Greek" style, which appealed to new collectors like the Prince de Condé, the son of the Duc de Bourbon. The commode which Leleu supplied for the Palais Bourbon in 1772 is a particularly fine example of this style; its design and its bronze furnishings using Graeco-Roman motifs. The dazzling marquetry is a reminder that marquetry had come back into fashion in the mid-eighteenth century.

The *marchands merciers* had to exploit the new style, as Poirier successfully did with the famous porcelain commode supplied to Madame du Barry in 1772. The olla from the Orloff service (1770–1771) shows how other techniques adopted the same trends as furniture.

The Louis XVI period retained the straight lines and antique-inspired decoration of the Greek style, but introduced greater lightness into the forms and mixed flowers and other figurative themes with the classical motifs. While the huge orders placed by the Garde-Meuble allowed the talent of Jean-Henri Riesener to develop to the full, with the secrétaire made for Marie-Antoinette at the Tuileries epitomizing its elegance, the *marchands merciers* were still powerful: the Darnault brothers were given the task of supplying lacquered furniture for the Château de Bellevue, while Dominique Daguerre who had succeeded Poirier supplied Marie-Antoinette's writing table at the Château de Saint-Cloud.

In the final years of the *ancien régime* the most original and sophisticated chairs of the period were made for Saint-Cloud including those by Séné. The queen loved music – the Sèvres bust of the "high priestess", probably alluding to Gluck's opera *Iphigénie en Aulide*, is a reminder of this – and collected *objets d'art*, such as the gold-mounted agate cassolette by her jeweller Charles Ouizille. The king bought many objects at the Duc d'Aumont's sale in 1782, including the antique serpentine covered cup which Pierre Gouthière had mounted in bronze, but he intended them for the Museum, which even then was under discussion.

Armchair "à la Reine"
Paris, c. 1710–1720
Made for Pierre Crozat (1661–1740),
Treasurer of France
Gilded walnut, morocco, red and white repp galloons
Height 110 cm; width 69 cm
Gift of Comte R.-H. de Caumont La Force, 1989
OA 11200

Commode
Ascribed to André-Charles Boulle (1642–1732)
Copper, pewter and tortoiseshell veneer on wooden core, gilt-bronze
Height 86 cm; width 148 cm
Transferred from the Mobilier National, 1901
OA 5477

The "Régent"
Diamond. 36 carats 7/8
Acquired for the Crown by the Regent,
Philippe d'Orléans, from Thomas Pitt,
Governor of Madras, in 1717
Formerly Crown Jewels (Diamants de la Couronne)
collection, assigned to the Louvre in 1887
MV 1017

Louis XV's crown
By Augustin Duflos (1715–1774),
after Claude Rondé, 1722
Partly gilded silver; facsimiles of precious
stones originally used (including the "Régent");
embroidered satin
Height 24 cm; diameter 22 cm
Deposited with the treasury of Saint-Denis in
1729 after the original precious stones had been
replaced, then at the Cabinet of Medals of the
Bibliothèque Nationale in 1793; at the Garde-
Meuble in the reign of Charles X, transferred
to the Louvre in 1852
MS 61

Snuff-box
Given to Louis Le Fort, Syndic of
Geneva, by Louis XV in 1727
By Daniel Govaers known as Gouers
(d. before 1754)
Paris, 1726–1727
Gold, diamonds, emeralds
Height 2.8 cm; width 8.2 cm
J. P. Getty gift, 1962
OA 10196

Mary Magdalene at the house of the Pharisee
First in the third set of tapestries based on
The New Testament, after Jouvenet (1711)
Paris, Gobelins factory, workshop of Lefebvre the younger,
1727
Tapestry, wool and silk
Height 513 cm; width 735 cm
Deposited by the Mobilier National, 1901
OA 5392

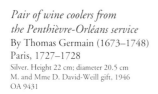

*Pair of wine coolers from
the Penthièvre-Orléans service*
By Thomas Germain (1673–1748)
Paris, 1727–1728
Silver. Height 22 cm; diameter 20.5 cm
M. and Mme D. David-Weill gift, 1946
OA 9431

Queen Marie Leczinska's "nécessaire"
By Henri-Nicolas Cousinet (d. c. 1768)
Paris, 1729-1730
Silver-gilt, ebony, porcelain
Given to the queen by Louis XV on the birth of the Dauphin
Gift of the Amis du Louvre with the participation of Mr St. Niarchos, 1955
OA 9598

Epergne of the Duc de Bourbon
By Jacques Röettiers (1707–1784)
Paris, 1736
Cast silver, chased. Height 62 cm; width 95 cm
Made for Louis-Henri, Duc de Bourbon,
Prince de Condé (1692–1740)
Acquired in 1976
OA 10631

Goldsmithing is one of the arts where the Rocaille style is best represented (thanks to the convergence of several techniques, such as casting, repoussé metal, chasing and engraving, which made anything possible). It pleased the inventive genius of Paris goldsmiths to transform table services into spectacular creations. The seals by Thomas Germain (from one of the most celebrated eighteenth-century sets of tableware belonging to the Penthièvre-Orléans family) are made to look like large shells with irregular, slightly spiralling ribs embellished with an exuberant naturalist decor of bunches of grapes and small molluscs, while the Röettiers epergne turns a utensil originally intended to serve as a tray into a bravura piece: four pillars of tortured rocks topped by a stag at bay and giving sanctuary to a trapped wolf rise from a terrace with curving feet (surrounded by boar's heads).

Bust on pedestal: Winter
Rouen, by Nicolas Fouquay (?),
c. 1735
Faience. Height 209 cm; width 60 cm
Formerly Duke of Hamilton's collection
Acquired in 1882
OA 2611

Story of Don Quixote:
the Barcelona ball
Paris, Gobelins factory, c. 1732–1736
After Charles Coypel (1694–1752)
Tapestry, wool and silk
Height 360 cm; width 505 cm
Dation in payment of inheritance taxes, 1978
OA 10664

The *Don Quixote* hangings are among the most beautiful produced at the Gobelins factory at the time of the French Regency and in the first years of Louis XV's reign; work started on the set inspired by Cervantes's novel in 1714. Pictures telling the story after models supplied by the painter Charles Coypel are set on large backgrounds ornamented with garlands – up to the time of the Revolution several copies were woven. The set held at the Louvre, the third to be woven at the Gobelins, was commissioned by Louis, Duc d'Orléans, as a gift for Comte d'Argenson; the duke's arms appear above the central picture while the count's are displayed at the sides. The distinguishing feature of this set is its superb pink ground.

Bureau plat
By Jacques Dubois (1694–1763)
Paris, c. 1745
Kingwood veneer on an oak and deal carcase,
gilt-bronze
Height 83 cm; width 197 cm
Transferred from the Ministry of Foreign Affairs,
1912
OA 6600

Commode
By Charles Cressent
(1685–1768)
Paris, c. 1730–1735
Amaranth
and satinwood veneer
on a deal and walnut carcase,
gilt-bronze,
purple breccia marble
Height 90.5 cm; width 149 cm
Gift of G. Ortiz
and J. Ortiz-Patiño, 1982
OA 10900

Commode
By Bernard II
Van Risen Burgh
(after 1696–c. 1766)
Paris, c. 1737
Fruitwood veneer,
Japanese lacquer
and vernis Martin
on an oak carcase,
gilt-bronze, Antin
(or Sarrancolin) marble
Height 85 cm; width 127 cm
Acquired in 1988
OA 1193

Clock "au chinois"
Paris, 1745–1749
Chased gilt-bronze. Height 55 cm
Transferred from the War Ministry,
1912
OA 6636

*Naiad known as
"la Source"*
Vincennes, 1756
Soft-paste porcelain,
gilt-bronze. Length 26 cm
Mme A. Thiers bequest,
1880
TH 693

*"Grand salon" of the Château d'Abondant
(Eure-et-Loir)*

Architecture by Jean Mansart de Jouy (d. after 1779),
joinery work by François-Simon Houlié (d. 1787),
paintings by Jacques de Sève, 1747-1750
Green-painted oak (woodwork, consoles) and beech (seats),
Sarrancolin marble, petit point tapestry
Created for Louis II du Bouchet, Marquis de Sourches (1711-1788)
Gift of the L. Lafon Laboratory, 1989
OA 11234 to 11248

There are hardly any surviving examples in France of eighteenth-century houses where the matching woodwork and furniture have been preserved. The furnishings of the "grand salon" of the Château d'Abondant are an exceptional reminder of this total concept of the interior decoration of a French château in the mid-eighteenth century: the console tables and armchairs match the carved panels, wainscotting, mirror piers and doors both in their dimensions and their decor, and the curves of the back rails of the sofas are shaped to correspond to the bottom rails supporting the mirrors above them.

Attempts were made to emulate the perfection of the works produced in Paris though they were never really matched either in
France or abroad, but there were sometimes strange time-lags.
The magnificent faience hanging wall-clock created in
Strasbourg c. 1750–1760 is obviously inspired by Parisian
bronzes used in furnishing at least a generation earlier: the figure
of Time with his scythe featured on the upper part and the two
women's busts on either side are in fact copied from the bronzes
created by Cressent on furniture made c. 1730–1740.

Hanging wall-clock
Strasbourg, Paul Hannong's
factory, c. 1750–1760
Faience. Height 112 cm; width 45 cm
I. de Camondo bequest, 1911
OA 6568

Andiron
By François-Thomas Germain (1726–1791)
Paris, 1757
Gilt-bronze, signed. Height 59 cm; length 60 cm
Acquired in 1935
OA 8278-8279

*Pot-pourri vase belonging
to Madame de Pompadour*
Sèvres, 1760
Soft-paste porcelain. Height 37 cm;
width 35 cm
Acquired in 1984
OA 10965

Armchair "à la Reine"
By Nicolas Heurtaut (1720–1771)
Paris, c. 1755
Gilded beech. Height 95 cm; width 62 cm
Made for Martial-Louis Beaupoil de Sainte-Aulaire,
Bishop of Poitiers (1759)
Acquired in 1975
OA 10594

The discovery of Herculaneum and Pompeii and publication of works relating to excavations there made decorative elements yet again derived from Greco-Roman Antiquity more widely known; from the mid-eighteenth century they contributed to a new artistic trend which was the precursor of Neo-Classicism. The use of curved forms and Rocaille decoration would continue up to the time of the Revolution, but from the 1760s in reaction straight lines, symmetrical swags, bucranes, sprays of piastres, fluting, claws and Greek key-pattern friezes appeared simultaneously in goldsmithing, furniture and bronzes used in furnishing.

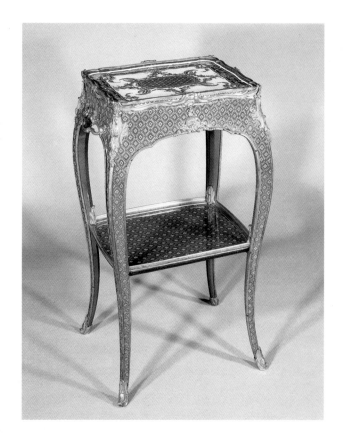

Chiffonnière
By Bernard II Van Risen Burgh
(after 1696–c. 1766)
Paris, c. 1764
Varnished fruitwood, soft-paste porcelain,
gilt-bronze
Height 66 cm
Fr. Guérault bequest, 1930
OA 8170

Prince de Condé's commode
By Jean-François Leleu (1729–1807)
Paris, 1772
Amaranth, tulipwood and sycamore veneer and
polychrome wood marquetry on an oak carcase,
gilt-bronze, red griotte marble
Height 87 cm; width 124.5 cm
Acquired in 1953
OA 9589

Olla from the Orloff service
By Jacques-Nicolas Röettiers
(1736–1788)
Paris, 1770–1771
Silver. Height 36 cm
Gift of the Amis du Louvre, 1933
OA 8246

Pair of "fish-tail" vases
Sèvres, c. 1765
Soft-paste porcelain. Height 38 cm
Gift of G. and P. Stern, 1983
OA 10916 and 10917

Vase with a siren and a female faun
Mount by Pierre Gouthière (1732–1813)
Paris, c. 1775–1780
Green porphyry, gilt-bronze
Height 38 cm; width 37 cm
Provenance, Duc d'Aumont's collections
Transferred from the Mobilier National, 1901
OA 5178

Cupid and Psyche
from *The loves of the god*
Paris, Gobelins factory, c. 1775
After Boucher and Jacques, by Neilson
Wool and silk tapestry
Height 425 cm; width 300 cm
Transferred from the Mobilier National, 1901
OA 5118

Madame Du Barry's
commode
Attributed to Martin
Carlin (1730–1785)
Paris, 1772
Pearwood, tulipwood and amaranth
veneer on an oak carcase,
soft-paste Sèvres porcelain plaques
(after Jean-Baptiste Pater,
Nicolas Lancret and Carle Van
Loo), gilt-bronze, white marble
Height 87 cm; width 119 cm
Dation in payment of capital
transfer taxes, 1990
OA 11293

Bust of the High Priestess
Sèvres, 1774
After a model by L.-S. Boizot
(1743-1809)
Soft-paste porcelain bisque.
Height 62.5 cm
M. and Mme G. Lefebvre gift, 1983
OA 10938

Vase
By the sculptor L.-S. Boizot
(1743–1809) and the bronzier
P.-P. Thomire (1751–1843)
Sèvres, 1783
Hard-paste porcelain, gilt-bronze
Height 200 cm
Formerly royal collections
OA 6627

The importance of the court and the personal role played by Queen Marie-Antoinette in royal commissions partly explain the extraordinary refinement of French cabinet-making in the reign of Louis XVI. It was at this juncture that some of the most remarkable pieces of furniture were created – remarkable for their opulent decoration of bronze mounts and marquetry applied to extremely sober forms, as in the pieces made by Riesener, the *ébéniste* who supplied the Crown until 1784. Furniture for everyday use such as writing tables was transformed by the fact that it was intended for royalty, as exemplified by the queen's costly writing table made by Weisweiler where the use of steel may be noted: a total novelty at the time.

Queen Marie-Antoinette's bureau à cylindre
By Jean-Henri Riesener (1734–1806)
Paris, 1784
Sycamore, amaranth and tulipwood veneer and polychrome wood marquetry,
gilt-bronze
Height 103.6 cm; width 113.4 cm
Transferred from the Mobilier National, 1901
OA 5226

Queen Marie-Antoinette's writing table
By Adam Weisweiler (1744–1820)
Paris, 1784
Ebony and sycamore veneer on an oak carcase,
Japanese lacquer, steel, gilt-bronze
Height 73.7 cm; width 81.2 cm
Transferred from the Mobilier National, 1870
OA 5509

Queen Marie-Antoinette's cassolette
By Charles Ouizille (1744–1830)
Paris, 1784–1785
Gold, agate, bloodstone, miniature behind glass
by Jacques-Joseph de Gault
Height 27.5 cm
Acquired in 1982
OA 10907

Cabriolet armchair
By Jean-Baptiste-Claude Séné (1747–1803)
Paris, 1787
Gilded walnut. Height 91 cm
Provenance, inner private room of Marie-Antoinette at Saint-Cloud
Transferred from the Mobilier National, 1948
OA 9452

The use of lacquers imported from the Far East became common in cabinet-making from the middle of the eighteenth century: caskets, cabinets and éscritoires were dismantled and if necessary cut up, then remounted on pieces furniture as decorative elements. One of the finest groups of furniture of this type, the pieces commissioned by Mesdames (Louis XV's daughters) for the Château de Bellevue, was the work of Martin Carlin: Madame Victoire's commode, which reuses parts of a seventeenth-century Japanese cabinet, is the culmination of the fashion for Orientalism combined with the ultimate sophistication of a decoration of gilt-bronze mounts which typified Parisian cabinet-making in the reign of Louis XVI.

Madame Victoire's commode
By Martin Carlin (1730–1785)
Paris, 1785
Ebony veneer and Japanese lacquer on an oak carcase,
gilt-bronze, white marble
Height 97 cm; width 150 cm
Transfer from the Mobilier National, 1870
OA 5498

The nineteenth century

Neoclassicism which had been fashionable throughout Europe for more than a quarter of century did not disappear in the wake of the upheaval occasioned by the French Revolution. But it possibly did have something to do with the emergence of furniture that was resolutely innovatory: the fact that it was so widely imitated afterwards obscures how extraordinary it was when it was first created. In 1798 the architect Louis-Martin Berthault was commissioned to furnish and decorate the house of the banker Jacques-Rose Récamier. He had been nurtured in the heroic antique culture which was then experiencing a revival and when he came to design furniture for Madame Récamier's bedroom, no doubt in collaboration with his great rival Charles Percier, he dreamt up a simply shaped bed with two symmetrical bed ends with scrolled back rests and a swan-shaped underframe embellished with gilt-bronze appliqué work inspired by Greek art, and a secrétaire and two tables de nuit decorated with female sphinxes following a similar concept based on elementary volumes. The furniture was probably made by the Jacob brothers, the most brilliant *ébénistes* of the period; it became widely known through engravings and was admired throughout Europe. Its lines made a decisive impact on Empire-style furniture which continued in a variety of forms well after the Empire had fallen. The seating in Madame Récamier's drawing-room with its antique appearance likewise ushered in a series of armchairs with armrests in the shape of female sphinxes and scrolled back rests, while the famous couch was immortalised by David in his portrait of Madame Récamier; of the drawing-room furniture only the guéridon bears the stamp of Jacob Frères.

Geometric volumes with pure lines were therefore used for Empress Josephine's monumental jewel-cabinet designed by Percier and made by the Jacob brothers in 1809; its luxury is supplied by gilt bronzes of the birth of Venus created by the sculptor Antoine-Denis Chaudet and mother-of-pearl inlaid work. Goldsmiths working in Paris during the Empire were inspired by a similar taste for Antiquity, Martin-Guillaume Biennais for example, who created a tea service for Napoleon I in 1810: Neptune and Amphitriton, winged victories, female sphinxes and elements borrowed from *The Aldobrandini Marriage* alternate in decorating the tea urn and the pieces that make up the service.

With the return of the Bourbons in 1815 Neoclassicism experienced a revival, as Charles X's state bed made by Brion supplied in 1824 illustrates; it favours straight lines and combines bold fleurs-de-lis, crested helmets, scrolls, palmettes, acanthus leaves and crowns of laurel. But underneath its seeming uniformity the Restoration sometimes demonstrated unexpected originality. For instance, the extravagant table de toilette belonging to the Duchesse de Berry designed by Marie-Jeanne-Rosalie Désarnaud-Charpentier c. 1819 is unique in combining crystal and gilt bronze on a metal frame, an innovative technique which, in its rejection of wood,

Ceiling cornice
Detail
Palais du Louvre,
"Grand salon"
of the Napoleon
III apartments

appears to anticipate the use of iron, steel and glass in architecture. Similarly the pair of vases given to Louis XVIII in 1817 by his brother, subsequently to become Charles X, designed in Sèvres using an already old model by the sculptor Clodion, are innovative in the way they bring together exotic subjects on the bulge, two elephants' tusks as handles and an Egyptian-inspired decoration on the foot: things Egyptian had been fashionable since the publication of Champollion's work.

Under the July Monarchy other trends contributed towards regenerating the decorative arts and prepared the ground for the advent of stylistic eclecticism in the second half of the century. Enthusiastic Historicism made its mark on furniture when the Grohé brothers brought back long-forgotten motifs from Renaissance art on the commode secrétaire of carved wood: female terms, strapwork and masks. A similar fascination with Renaissance gold and silver explains the inventive spirit behind the Wine Harvest Cup, designed and made by Froment-Meurice, Jules Wièse and Antoine Vechte c. 1844, while the Orientalism which was soon to become fashionable is already apparent in the amazing reticulate Chinese breakfast service belonging to Queen Marie-Amélie, made at Sèvres in 1840.

In theory the art of the Second Empire and the late nineteenth century has been relocated at the Musée d'Orsay since 1986. However, the reliquary brooch belonging to Empress Eugénie with two of Mazarin's diamonds set in it, kept out of the sale of the Crown Jewels in 1887 because of this, has of course remained on display beside the Crown Jewels in the Galerie d'Apollon. The empress's crown joined them in 1988; it was made by Alexandre-Gabriel Lemonnier, jeweller to the Crown, to mark the 1855 Universal Exhibition at which Napoleon III displayed some of the Crown Jewels which had recently been reset. The crown made for the emperor at the same time has been destroyed.

Finally, the fact that the Richelieu wing, which used to house the Ministry of Finance, was transferred to the Museum in 1989 has given the Louvre a matchless set of Second Empire State Apartments, the finest of their type in France. They were furnished between 1856 and 1861, under the supervision of the architect Hector Lefuel, to serve as a residence for the Minister of State, Achille Fould. The keynote is sumptuousness: while inspired by the century of Louis XIV the art is eclectic, both in the stately furniture and the grand decor of stucco work, paintings and panelling, not to mention the magnificence of the crystal chandeliers.

Madame Récamier's bed
By Jacob Frères: Georges II Jacob
(d. 1803) and François-Honoré-Georges
known as Jacob-Desmalter (1770–1841)
Paris, c. 1798
Mahogany and gilt-bronze
Length 201 cm; width 133 cm
Gift of the Amis du Louvre, 1991
OA 11344

Madame Récamier's drawing room
By Jacob Frères
Paris, c. 1798
Walnut construction with veneer of bois d'espénille
(from San Domingo), amaranth, mahogany, ebony and satinwood
Gift of M. and Mme. V. Pastor, 1994
OA 11383-11391

"Clodion" vase (one of a pair)
Painted decoration by Charles
Develly (1783–1849)
Sèvres, 1817
Porcelain. Height 76 cm
Given to the Comte d'Artois, subsequently
Charles X, by Louis XVIII
Acquired in 1991
OA 11340

Napoleon I's tea service
By Martin-Guillaume Biennais
(1764–1843)
Paris, 1809–1810
Silver-gilt. Height (urn): 80 cm
Acquired in 1951
OA 9537

*Empress
Josephine's
jewel-cabinet*
By François-
Honoré-Georges
Jacob known as
Jacob-Desmalter
from drawings by
Percier and
Chaudet; bronze
mounts by
Thomire
Paris, 1809
Veneer of yew (from the
islands) and amaranth on
an oak carcase, mother-of-
pearl, gilt-bronze
Height 276 cm
Deposit from the National
Museum of the Château
de Fontainebleau, 1964
OA 10245

Bed of Charles X
By Pierre-Gaston Brion (b. 1767)
Gilded wood. Height 220 cm; length 240 cm
Transferred from the Mobilier National, 1965
OA 10278

Eighteenth-century *ébénistes* were extremely innovative in their choice of materials, introducing porcelain or – like Weisweiler for example – steel into their works. Marie-Jeanne-Rosalie Désarnaud followed in the wake of these pioneers with the table de toilette and accompanying arm-chair that belonged to the Duchesse de Berry, opening up new avenues by doing away with the use of wood and exploring the effects of transparency and the brilliancy of crystal. These extraordinary pieces created at the time of the Restoration adhere in their broad lines to the Empire style, in the bronze figures of Flora and Zephyr surrounding the table mirror in particular, yet in a strange way they anticipate some items of contemporary furniture.

Table de toilette
By Marie-Jeanne-Rosalie Désarnaud-
Charpentier (1775–1842)
and Nicolas-Henri Jacob
(1782–1871)
Paris, c. 1819
Crystal, verre églomisé, gilt-bronze
Height 171 cm
C. Ott gift with the help of M. M. Segoura,
1989
OA 11229-11230

Wine harvest cup
By François-Désiré
Froment-Meurice (1802–1855)
Paris, c. 1844
Partly gilded and enamelled silver,
agate, pearls
Height 35 cm
Acquired in 1984
OA 11011

Commode-secrétaire
By Guillaume Grohé
(1808–1885)
Paris, 1839, signed and dated
Rosewood, ebony, palm wood, marble
Height 100 cm; width 120 cm
Gift of the Amis du Louvre, 1988
OA 11197

Empress Eugénie's crown
By Alexandre-
Gabriel Lemonnier (1808–1884)
Paris, c. 1855
Gold, diamonds and emeralds
Height 13 cm; diameter 15 cm
Made for the empress on the occasion
of the 1855 Universal Exhibition
M. and Mme R. Polo gift, 1988
OA 11160

Queen Marie-Amélie's "reticulated
Chinese" breakfast service
Sèvres, 1840
Hard-paste porcelain. Height 29.5 cm
J.-M. Rossi gift, 1986
OA 11098-11111

Napoleon III apartments
"Grand salon", 1856–1861
After Hector-Martin Lefuel (1810–1882);
models of sculptures by Louis-Alphonse Tranchant
(b. 1822) and painted decoration by
Laurent-Jan Lausanne (1809–1877)

Napoleon III apartments
Small dining-room, interior decoration
carried out under the supervision of
Hector-Martin Lefuel
and Laurent-Jan Lausanne

INDEX

Figures in Roman typeface refer to pages on which the proper names are mentioned; figures in bold italics refer to reproductions of the works.

PHOTOGRAPHIC ACKNOWLEDGMENTS

Éditions Fatton : pp. 102b, 108, 109, 118, 119

Louvre, Department of Objets d'Art : cover (Beck Coppola) and p. 106 (Beck Coppola)

Réunion de Musées nationaux : endpapers and pp. 6, 14, 17hg, 17hd, 17b (Arnaudet), 18, 19h, 19b (Arnaudet), 20 (Arnaudet), 23 (Chuzeville), 24h (Arnaudet), 24b, 25h, 25b (Arnaudet), 26 (Arnaudet), 27, 28 (Arnaudet), 31, 32 (Arnaudet), 33h (Arnaudet), 33b, 34h (Arnaudet), 34m (Arnaudet), 34b, 35 (Arnaudet), 36 (Arnaudet), 37hg, 37hd (Arnaudet), 37b (Arnaudet), 38g, 38d (Beck Coppola), 39h (Arnaudet), 39b (Beck Coppola), 40g, 40hd (Arnaudet), 41 (Arnaudet), 42, 43 (Arnaudet), 44g (Arnaudet), 44d, 45, 46, 47g (Arnaudet), 47d, 48, 49, 50, 53h, 53b (Arnaudet), 54, 55h (Arnaudet), 55b, 56, 57, 58 (Arnaudet), 59g (Arnaudet), 59d, 60 (Chuzeville), 61h, 61b (Arnaudet), 62, 65, 66h, 66b (Arnaudet), 67, 68, 69h (Arnaudet), 70, 71, 72, 73, 74, 77hg (Arnaudet), 77d, 77bg (Arnaudet), 78g, 78d (Arnaudet), 79 (Arnaudet), 80h, 80b (Arnaudet), 81, 82h, 82b (Chuzeville), 83, 84, 85 (Arnaudet), 86 (Arnaudet), 89 (Arnaudet), 90, 91h, 91b (Arnaudet), 92, 93, 94, 95 (Beck Coppola), 96h, 96b (Arnaudet), 97, 98h (Arnaudet), 98b, 99, 100, 101h (Arnaudet), 101b, 102, 103h (Arnaudet), 103b, 104h, 104b (Arnaudet), 105, 107, 110g (Arnaudet), 110d, 111 (Chuzeville), 113, 114h, 114b (Beck Coppola), 116 (Arnaudet), 117h (Arnaudet), 117b (Chuzeville), 120, 121h, 121b (Arnaudet), 122, 123

Printed in Italy by Graphicom
Colour separation by Daïchi Process - Singapore
Dépôt légal: november 1995